MW01181200

The Incredible World of:

Gold Rush Ghosts

True Stories of Hauntings
in the Mother Lode

By

Nancy Bradley
TBR

ISBN: 1-57502-801-8

Library of Congress Catalog Card Number: 98-92845

10   9   8   7   6   5   4   3   2   1

Published By:
Morris Publishing
3212 Hwy. 30
Keamey, NE 68847

Dedicated To:

My wonderful sounding board, friend, and mentor, my Dad, William H.Bradley, and my children, the best ever, Bob, Robin and Shannon King, and my Granddaughter, and pal, the Shu-She Woman. I love you.

The Incredible World Of
GOLD RUSH GHOSTS

True Stories of Hauntings
in
The Mother Lode

By

NANCY BRADLEY
TBR

Cover Photo By: DAVE NOVICK
Photos By: DANIEL AMOS
                  ROBERT REPPERT
Cover Design: DANIEL AMOS
Design Management:DANIEL AMOS
Map By: ROBERT REPPERT

Editorial Management:
ROBERT REPPERT

Cover Photo: One   of   the   many   settler
graveyards overlooking the gold fields and
1800 buildings in the Mother Lode of Calif.

Back Cover : The staff of Gold Rush Ghosts,
Dan Amos, Nancy Bradley & Robert Reppert.

ACKNOWLEDGMENTS

First and foremost, much thanks must go to the business owners, store employees, landlords, historians, experts, long time Gold Rush Country residents, and all the folks who's stories are represented here, for their gracious time and help in my getting the facts correct, as I put this book together. We have become great friends over this process, and they were kind enough to allow me into their lives at all ungodly times, without complaint. Thanks must also go to the psychics who gave tirelessly to the completion of this work, by name, Pat Kenyon, and my long time dear friend Rosemary Dean, two truly gifted psychics in a world of phonies. Thru them many mysteries, and spirits that wanted to leave were put to rest.

To my Dad, William H.Bradley, my brothers, William Bradley and Michael Bradley, and my sister Mary Bradley. Thank you for your unfailing help, for going way beyond the call of family duty to protect me and get me out of the horror that was my life. Without you I would still be a victim. They have said I am made of steel to have survived, but it was their backbones, checkbooks, expertise, guts and encouragement I leaned on. You never let me down, and let me say now I love you, because sometimes we forget to do so.

Thanks to my children Bob, Robin and Shannon King and my granddaughter Shu She for their great outlooks, support, and love, to the two Ishmaels, and to Kimberly DELANE who's 1-800-Insult Hotline has kept me, as it would anyone, well grounded. Love ya.

I am also grateful for my wonderful friend of nine years, Bear dog, a 110 lb. Chesapeake Bay Retriever who never left my side even if I was writing till dawn. To

my friend and soul mate, Vincent Gaddis, a
fellow author and co-author, who knew there
were broken wings, and mended them with love
and encouragement because he believed in my
talent even when I was not so sure. And, of
course, my two friends since high school
Larry Corona and Linda Cryer Netherton,
because I love you both as much today as I
did back then. Its amazing how we still can
manage to get in so much trouble. We will go
down in history, for nothing can defeat the
gruesome threesome. To Robert, my undying
love.

But no more can be said without
acknowledging the folks who's lives and
incredible stories made it all possible,
specifically the spirits and specters of the
1800's, that continue to make things go
bump, even today.

"There is only a single supreme idea on earth: the concept of immortality of the human soul; all other profound ideas, by which men live, are only an extension of it."

   -Fyodor Dostoevsky (1821-1881), in _Diary of a Writer_

CONTENTS

PREFACE

This is a book about ghosts, specifically the uncanny number of apparitions that haunt the Mother Lode Country of California. It was while investigating ghost stories for a National Magazine that the author noticed the Gold Rush Country had six times the number of sightings in comparison to other parts of the country, including New England, well known for its many hauntings. She then researched countries across our world known to have excessive, yet credible, stories of ghosts, such as Ireland, Wales, and England. The Mother Lode topped them five to one in territory and time frame.

But what are ghosts? Should they be feared? Why do we see them? Why do they hover in the Gold Country?

The author is convinced there are three types of ghosts or sightings of the deceased. Some are earthbound spirits, bound to the environment they knew in physical life by habits, emotions or desire. They are, perhaps, lost souls, caught in the web of time.

There are those who appear out of "earth memory", or what is called "akashic records" in oriental philosophy. Simply said, everything we do is imprinted in time. These spirits are no longer here, perhaps, but we are, in fact, tapping into another time when they were, and seeing their actions at that time. Like a motion picture, the apparitions in these visions endlessly repeat, over and over again, some event that was emotionally charged. These phantasms, seem to be portraying an aspect of the daily life that the spirit they represent experienced in physical life.

The third is the "in and out" spirit, who, (often times we knew them in this lifetime), comes to warn of troubles, or just to hang with us. They appear to come into our world and be a part of the hereafter as well. There are many other variations of all ghost explanations, and combinations of such. Another book dealing with just this subject is in the works.

It is not surprising that many, many, ghosts dwell in the gold country. It was a time of charged energy, a place of violence and greed. Thousands lost their lives abruptly and "before their time." Here the past equates with the present. Some may want to continue what they started. Others perhaps, because they died before they were ready to do so, don't know how to, or at least don't want to, get to the other side. You can feel it all around you, in the streets, old buildings, cemeteries, and mountains. Some seem to be calling for help, asking for direction. Others may wish to stay, and some ask closure.

Yes, there are many ghosts in the Gold Rush Country of California, and here are the incredible stories of some of them.

SUTTER'S MILL
Let The Exodus Begin

On January 24th, 1848, an event was to happen so magical, so unanticipated, so phenomenal, and so earth shattering that it was to change the course of history for a full nation, and forever change the lives of half the population.

On this fateful crisp day in the tiny hamlet of Coloma in Northern California, James W. Marshall, a skilled carpenter and partner with John A. Sutter in a sawmill, looked down into the tailrace to notice two small nuggets in the water. He scooped them up and put them into his pocket. "Men" he said excitedly to his crew, "If these are what I think they are, we are all going to be rich!" He happily pulled them from his pocket and showed them around.

Marshall's partner, John Sutter was skeptical. "Probably fool's gold" he told the men. "Iron pyrites look just like gold. Pyrites are brittle and gold is more soft." He demanded they make the standard tests before passing the rumor. The following day the two men pounded the nuggets, heated them, boiled them in lye, and dropped them in acid. The doubter shook hands with the founder. They had GOLD!

Sutter, always the more rational of the two men, insisted they keep quiet about the

find until the mill was finished. Still
under construction, he needed the lumber,
but it was to be Sutter himself who broke
the agreement. He told his friend, Sam
Brannan, an elder in the Mormon Church about
the find. Brannan immediately went to the
mill and collected tithe from all who worked
there and were members of the Mormon
Battalion. A storekeeper by trade, Brannan
passed the news on when he went to San
Francisco to change the gold into currency
for forwarding to the Mormon headquarters in
Salt Lake City. He paraded the streets of
San Francisco, waving a quinine bottle
containing the gold, and shouting "Gold,
Gold, from the American River." Within days
almost every man in San Francisco had
hurried to the gold fields. The fever spread
throughout the country and abroad as homes
and shops were abandoned, crops were left
unharvested and newspapers suspended
publication. What businesses remained were
primarily conducted by women, as their men
set out to make the fortunes. They left
behind trails of broken wagon parts, lonely
graves, bleached animal bones, and an easier
life. Between 1847 and 1850 the population
of California increased from 15,000 to
92,497. A decade later the U.S. Census
enumerated 379,994 persons in the State.

Some came, not to look for gold, but to
provide services, or to prey on the tired
miners. There were gamblers and prostitutes,
store-minders and saloon-keepers. Operators
of general stores became very wealthy, an
egg, for example, could easily sell for five
dollars. It is told the prostitutes were the
wealthiest in the Gold Country, but few
remained "Ladies of the evening" for very
long. Because women were a rare commodity,
most either became wives of the more
prosperous, or took their new found gain and
returned to the east better off than they

2

started.

Naturally with such an environment of sudden wealth and greed, crime was quick to raise it's ugly head. Claim jumping, card sharking, excessive drinking and unclear heads caused a barrage of crimes, and punishment was swift, a knife in the gut, a shot to the head. Several hangings a day were not uncommon.

Meanwhile, back in the gold fields, the men searched for the elusive metal. It's worth repeating. GOLD! In the earlier days they fanned out from their tents and leantos in boisterous shanty towns with names such as; RedDog, You Bet, Angel's Camp, Git-Up-and-Get, Bogus Thunder, Shinbone Creek, and Lazy Man's Canyon. In those days they could find nuggets on the surface. Sometimes gold was picked out of the rock "as fast as one can pick kernels out of a lot of well-cracked shell barks." One trench 100 feet long yielded its two owners $17,000 in seven days, a hefty profit in those days.

Some of the miners managed to keep their fortunes, but most who were able to escape with their lives went home nearly empty handed.

From the standpoint of material possessions, Sutter lost the most. Before the gold rush, he had an agricultural empire. Then came Sutter's armageddon. Gold hungry prospectors overran his land, stole his cattle, drove off his Indians, and, winningly, challenged his rights to his land. In 1873 he gave up his struggle and moved to Pennsylvania with only a small pension for his services in the Mexican War. In 1880 he died in Washington D.C. after an unsuccessful bid to Congress to restore his property and increase his pension.

The end result was not much better for Marshall. He to would suffer for his find. On the strength of his gold find he attempted to claim a part of the Coloma Valley. Gold-seekers posted armed guards around their diggings to keep him out. His presence was considered bad luck, and friends, judges, juries, and even his lawyers turned against him. Friendless, he died on August 10, 1885 in Kelsey, a small community about fifteen miles 'as the crow flies' from Coloma. In his hand was his last solace, whiskey. Only then did the miners choose to remember he was responsible for the original gold find, and packing his body in ice, drove him by wagon to his final resting place in Coloma, overlooking the trailrace where a beautiful monument was erected over his grave to honor him.

Today the spot is part of the 18 acre Marshall Gold Discovery State Historic Park, which also houses a recreation of the original sawmill, several old gold rush stores, a very informative museum with artifacts of the era, and our Marshall's Monument. Although it is the final resting place of James Marshall, he does not choose to stay buried in his plot. Although a statue of him atop the monument points in the direction of his gold find, often a filmy shadow of a man is seen behind it, holding something long and defined in it's hand. Many visitors to the site think they have the answer to this unexplainable quivering shadow. "It is Marshall" they have told the author. "Still holding that bottle of whiskey." You are now in Marshall Gold Discovery State Park. Enjoy, as you begin your step into ghost country.

<u>BELL'S</u> <u>GENERAL</u> <u>STORE</u>
Where past customers specters still linger

The long gone bell is part of the mystery. The building is falling apart from the ravages of time and carelessness. Most certainly it is beyond repair, and will never be used again.

But in 1850 it was the only general store for miles around, and rather than trek to San Francisco where prices were reasonable, most miners chose to (literally) bite the bullet and pay the prices of one Robert Bell, to quickly secure their supplies, and get back to the business of gold seeking. They had little choice, and Bell knew it. He sold potatoes for $1.00 each, and a bottle of whiskey for $10.00. If you wanted to sit in his store and drink it, he would also be willing to help you empty the bottle. You might just then buy another. Many decisions concerning the community were settled over a bottle in Bell's store, among the clattering of canned goods, the dragging of horses hay, and pouring from barrels of dry goods. Bell was a shrewd businessman, with a bell over the door to announce a customer with money to spend. He was in control. He was happy. And he got richer than most of the miners he sold too.

Years passed, the Gold Rush era eased into books about history, and the building went from stately to eye-sore. Bell died, and so did the miners, but the sales and commotion in the store continued, as it does to this day. For folks who live around the park, and some who travel through at night, the bell continues to ring. That is, the spectral bell. As we said before, the 'other' one is long gone.

"I feel a man here" stated gifted world renown psychic Rosemary Dean to the author on a special trip to Marshall Gold Discovery Park. We had come in the early morning of November, 1997, to find the truth about the ghost rumors. In a world full of phonies, Rosie had been tested by the masters. She seeks no publicity, and has a spotless record for truthfulness and accuracy. Formed through years of friendship, we felt gifted that she was willing to take time from her work with police investigations and private practice to accompany us. With tape recorder in hand we were comfortable knowing she would have us print nothing but what she found to be actually present. That is a gift, indeed, as many ghost books are plagued with rumors and make-believe. We had chosen not to be one of them.

"At the time of the Gold Rush, Robert Bell hired a young man to help tend the store" Rosie told us. "He is somewhere between the ages of 18 and perhaps 25. He has a cowlick in the back of his head, and his hair stands straight up in that spot. He spits on his hand and puts it to his head to try and plaster it down, but it doesn't help." Rosie smiled as she repeated the actions of the young man. "He helps scoop dry goods from the barrels, sugar, flour and beans. He helps with the livestock supplies and the clean up as well. There appears to be a long wooden counter from which alcohol is served and other items purchased, kind of a cashier's place. Bell is working it. The young man's name is Timothy, and there is another man about the same age in the store by the name of Jonathan. I see a crusty old codger called Harold. Harold is a kind of fixture in the store, always hanging around.

If he can start some verbal trouble "He will" Rosie was to tell us. "He loves a good fight. I see yarn, oats, shovels in the corner, and rope and twine."

In the 'old days', Bell's Store was one of only two brick buildings in the area. Before crumbling, it also served as a Post Office. "I don't see any postal employees around here" Rosie said, "The ghosts are all from the merchandise store days."

Late at night on June 7th, 1997 Bill and Clara Feldman and their daughter Mona* were traveling thru the park on their way to Placerville. "It was about 2:00 A.M., and we heard a bell sounding in the vicinity of the river" Bill Feldman told the author. "Figuring it was probably coming from a rafting camp or trailer area near by, we stopped to satisfy our curiosity. The sound was coming from behind the old abandoned building called Bell's Store. Well, I thought some kids might be fooling around, so I took my flashlight from the trunk and went to investigate. The sound stopped abruptly. I circled the building with the light, and there was no one around." Feldman said he then returned to his car. "As we drove off we could hear the bell ring again, and Clara and Mona both said they saw a shadow about six foot off the ground go thru the closed and locked door to the building. I did not go back to investigate."

"There is also a woman who sells her services here" Rosie admitted. "She is wearing a long satin two piece dress, long gloves, and a round hat with a feather in it. She has brown hair and her name is Agnes (Aggy). "She does not actually do her work

NOTE: An * after a name indicates we are using another name, respecting the privacy of the person involved.

at Bell's, but, 'ahem' ,solicits business from there. She is a lady of the evening for sure, but another spirit, Ellen, older than Aggy yet dressed very much the same, stands beside her. There is also a large woman here, Rebecca by name, who wears a mans shirt with the sleeves rolled up and a long skirt. She is not being very pleasant to either Aggy or Ellen. Aggy thinks it's hilarious, amusing actually. She mocks Rebecca, because she considers the woman a joke."

And so the specters of the past still inhabit Bell's store in the present, although their physical bodies have returned to the earth. These bodies could be buried anywhere over the foothills, in the fields and in the cemeteries. But their spirits roam, happily, carelessly, effortlessly, here.

For the adventurous, the ghosts, shadows, and ringing bell at this site is best experienced at night when all seems asleep in darkness. It is then that non-believers find it hard to explain what they wish they had not seen and heard. Mark Twain called it the "Greater realities. This world is but a reflection of the real realms that lie beyond our ken" he wrote. Those who have experienced the exceptional phenomena at Bell's General Store know exactly what he means.

THE ARGONAUT
THE OLD SCHULZE HOUSE
AND DOCTOR TAYLOR'S OFFICE
A House With Spooks And
A Field with Memories

In November and December of 1997 a group of student Archaeologists from the California State University in Sacramento roped away areas of Marshall Gold Discovery State Park on highway 49 in Coloma. They worked around a plaque, placed to commemorate a historic spot where as early as 1849, one dedicated man, Doctor William Taylor, ran a hospital, drug store, and pharmacy. The doctor meticulously kept a complete line of the latest available drugs, chemicals, acids and extracts. He set bones, treated colds, flu, pneumonia, and the many other maladies of the day. He became increasingly frustrated as the cold winters held a death grip on the newborn, and the wounded men with pans and shovels depended on their comrades to get them to his office when an accident happened. If the argonauts were in the midst of a gold find, the injured was often the last priority. Many an unfortunate miner, brought to the 'Doc' too late for repair, gave up his physical life at Doctor Taylor's Hospital. With the frenzy of getting back to the hills and streams, and the cold reality of breaking hard ground in the winter, did the miners sometimes deter burials for their buddies until a later date? Were bodies stashed away or buried haphazardly until a proper burial time could be arranged? We don't know. But the place where Doctor Taylor had his hospital is only a field now. Archaeologists are searching there for bottles, bones, and anything else of interest to historians. Do they suspect

9

more? Some have inquired about our investigation.

We are concentrating on the old Schulze House next door to the empty field where they are working. Though built after the gold rush days, the ghostly phenomena experienced at the building is worthy of investigating.

Built as a home for his daughter Daisy in 1916, Charles Schulze sat back and admired his work. In the late 1800's he was well known in Coloma as a blacksmith, a miner, a teamster and mason. Although his daughter did not live in Coloma, she did visit from time to time, and he wanted her comfortable. In 1886 he inherited the Sierra Nevada House down the street, and became a hotel keeper. He wanted the home he built for her to give her privacy and a place to enjoy and entertain. When he died in 1921, and after her death as well, the house was used as a residence for his heirs.

But back to the present, for the last six years the Schulze home has been used as a restaurant, coffee house, and all around social meeting place for local folk and weary travelers. Called The Argonaut the business is owned by old friends Silvia Hlavacek and Debbie Zemanek. Because Debby is off with other adventures, it is most likely Silvia who will greet you at the place. Friendly and outgoing, she is happy to tell you her experiences with the unknown, and those of her housekeeper, in this charming old house.

"It's the footsteps I hear that have become annoying" she told us. "I will be working in the back of the store and hear someone come in the front. I holler out 'Be right there', complete what I am doing, and race for the front to find no one in the place. This happens quite often. I have no answer for it, but it gives you a weird

10

feeling."

Psychic Rosemary Dean picked up on one spirit immediately. "There is a wash woman here" she told us. "Her name is Alice. Everyone seems busy to her and they do not pay attention to her. She comes here because she likes the smells, especially the coffee and espresso. She is a large woman and has a square face. She wishes someone would just acknowledge her. She is not a mean spirit, just lonely."

Dianne Parrish of Placerville tells of her experience in the building. "I saw an older man walk over and stand at the window. He looked out, watching the trees. He was fat, and had grey hair and was wearing overalls. He seemed filmy when I saw him, not really transparent, but I knew something was weird about him. Then he just slowly disappeared." She held my hand. "I was afraid to tell anyone about him until now. I thought maybe I was losing my mind."

"My housekeeper has a story to tell you" Sylvia was to share with us. "One morning when she came in to clean, she saw a ghost. She was dressed in a long dress and it was a light blue color. She looked around, confused, and then disappeared. Actually, she has complained of seeing her more than once."

As it turns out, she is probably the entity that calls herself Helen. Rosie was to pick her up immediately. "She was very familiar with this part of the community in the late 1800's, and is of English extraction. I see her with 'boxed lunches', sort of an outing, a picnic type of event that is taking place on the green. I don't think she is aware there is a house here. She is just going to the picnic."

Before we left, Rosie was to ask to go under the house to the cellar. Once there, one of our photographers felt dizzy, his

teeth began to hurt, and he insisted on
exiting the building. I entered with Rosie
and two companions, Peggy and Danette Hogan.
We walked past the end of the floorboards
to an ancient door. We opened it to find a
space under the house made of just piers
and with a dirt bottom. It was big enough to
walk into, and so we did. I felt light
headed and put my hand against one of the
piers for balance. Rosie looked at me with
information that would soon astound the
owner. "There are bodies buried here" She
told us. "They have been here a very long
time. Some of the entities are staying here
at the house and surrounding property. It is
a solemn time, as they should have been
buried elsewhere."

As we left the crawl space I told Rosie
of my theory about Dr. Taylor's patients.
Could they be buried here, next to his
hospital, and the house erected over their
graves?

We then went back into the house to tell
Sylvia that we suspected bodies were buried
under The Argonaut.

Did Dr. Taylor bury winter unfortunates
under the old Schulze House?

"That is strange" she was to tell us. "The archaeologists asked to go under the building to the crawl space too. They came back with a piece of metal and asked me where it came from. I told them it came up out of the ground when we were flooded last winter." She looked at us intently. "They asked me if I knew what it was and I had to admit I did not. They said 'Well, it's a handle off an old coffin'".

Sylvia and The Argonaut are a real treat if you get to Marshall Gold Discovery State Park. She is open for business from 10:00 a.m. to 5:00 p.m., March through mid-December. It's the friendliest place in town, with amazing stories to tell.

WAH LEE (Man Lee) STORE
Prospering Outside the Gold Fields

The Chinese also saw an opportunity. They migrated to the Mother Lode by the thousands. They brought to the gold country their lifetime beliefs and customs, which were looked upon as strange, disturbing, and annoying. The miners originally brought them here to provide cheap labor, not to search for gold which several of them branched out to do. Their culture was different than the fast living miners. The Chinese were frugal. Many of them skimped, and sent their money back home to their families in China. Few added to the local economy. The high-living, fast-lane prospectors made fun of them, mocked them, and watched them with interest. Very few of the Chinese drank, gambled, or visited the cat-houses. They kept to themselves, but were still persecuted, discriminated against, and without proper cause, hated.

It was in Coloma that the worst racial incident occurred in 1861 after Henry Mahler did the unthinkable by selling the ground where his former hotel had stood to a company of Chinese. According to Mary Edith Crosley, in her book Coloma , the Chinese began mining the land, which had also been claimed by a group of Irishmen as vacant mining property. The leader of the Irish, James O'Donnell, took it to the courts. The courts ruled in favor of the Chinese, but the Irish vowed to dispossess them, by force if necessary.

They met at the bar in Bell's store where they proceeded to get intoxicated. With alcoholic bravado, they marched noisily to the claim and drove the Chinese away.

"Lets go chink hunting and chase the yellow-bellies out of town for good," shouted O'Donnell.

They returned to the store where they added to their whiskey consumption. Then, author Crosley continues, "They headed down Main Street toward Chinatown, where they went on a rampage, wrecking and destroying everything they could lay their hands on. What they did not destroy, they stole. The frightened Chinese who managed to escape with their lives went into hiding. A few were killed outright and many were seized and badly beaten."

The town Constable was outnumbered. Alone he could not break up the mob. Drunk and rowdy, they were out for blood, and paid no attention to his threats. The officer raced to a building where he found a pad and pencil, and wrote down the names of the rioters he could remember and identify. A brave man, the following day he made sixteen arrests, placing the hung-over troublemakers in jail. He crossed their names off his list as they were found, and then went out searching for the next. News of the arrests

14

traveled fast, and the rest of yesterdays mob, sober now, knew they were in trouble. Many went into hiding, and fearing their fate, even more left the area for good.

The sixteen were convicted, and fined $200 each. Several spent nearly all summer in jail before their friends or families could (or wanted to) raise the money to pay their fines. In the blistering heat of Coloma this could not have been a comfortable fate.

The industrious Chinese, undaunted, continued to work long hours and were satisfied to rework gold claims abandoned as worthless by other miners. Long after most miners fanned out to other parts of the Mother Lode country, the Chinese were still finding color around Coloma. They were the last of the prospectors to leave. One hard working Chinese gentleman, however, had another dream. He chose to forfeit any claims in the gold fields. He chose to run a store.

Wah Lee had an astonishing repertoire of merchandise. The year was 1858, and he leased a store built by white settlers. He sold groceries, prospecting supplies, meats, hardware, clothing, furniture, exotic Chinese teas, health cures from the orient, spices and Chinese dishes. Some have said the wily Lee sold other things as well. We don't know this for sure, because there apparently were no complainers.

But please follow us now into the cold, disturbing store that was Wah Lee's, now a museum. The interior is protected by a grill, but still visible. We look around and feel uneasy with the heavy air inside the building. Breathing labored, we realize we can hear nothing but the birds outside in the locust trees.

Paradisiacal phenomena cannot be turned on like an electrical switch. The psychic realm has its own laws that we don't fully understand. We try to be patient. There are thousands of lives that these aged walls have known. How many still remain?

All should be still. But at night the park is dark, and we have heard about the sounds that pervade the cracks and interstices of this old building. In this silent world, suddenly unnatural sounding voices chill us frightfully. We have tapped into lives that have advanced into the unknown, leaving their spirits confused and haunting. Yes, we now hear it, slowly becoming louder. It is the merged murmur of many voices, faintly rising and falling in volume in response to some strange impulse. We look at each other, our eyes filled with wonder in the presence of the great unknown. The chill of musty bodies, dead in our world a long time, pass through our bodies. The steady cadence continues and becomes louder. It is in Chinese and English, as the store served Caucasian as well. Now we determine the loudest of the broken voices are that of an oriental man and woman, calling from long ago, humming the music of their motherland, as an invisible cleaver chops at a wooden block. Wah Lee? Perhaps. But the sounds that come in the night are from someone, somewhere, from long ago...........

Soon the sounds begin to fade, slowly, back into mysterious time-space, the warp from whence it came. Then it is gone. The building is silent once more and we again are listening only to the birds outside the store. We step outside and know we have been gifted by this experience. We are walking away from the world of the vastly deep, back to ours of prosaic daily life. Our experience may have seemed like a dream. But it was not..............

THE MARSHALL MONUMENT
Strange Spectral Shadows

Overlooking the park, in its overpowering way, is the bronze, larger-than-life statue of James Marshall. It is high atop a granite pedestal. One of his hands points toward the spot where he made his great discovery. The other over his heart. The statue was erected over his grave in 1890, a memorial. It is here we would expect James Marshall to rest, through time and history. But he does not.

We feel it is fitting and proper that one of the best affirmations of ghosts in our survey of gold rush apparitions should be of James Marshall himself. Here where he was remembered and honored at last, he chooses to mingle with park visitors." Do you see what I have done?" He seems to be asking. He has returned from the dark realm of shadows of the dead, to enjoy the recognition and prestige that were denied him in his physical life.

Marshall believed in the hereafter. He insisted he had spirit friends to guide him. He told his drinking companions that the spirits promised to lead him to rich gold deposits.

He should not have shared this information. When he felt their inspiration, Marshall would start walking where his spirit friends guided him. He was invariably followed by frustrated greedy fortune seekers who believed in these supernormal powers. Unfortunately but invariably, and perhaps because Marshall's guide's did not want to share this information, the group generally ended up in locations that had already been worked over by earlier miners.

Even when the spirits gave correct information, it did not matter. When Marshall stalked out a claim, his pursuers staked claims around his, pushing their limits. If there was any gold there, his followers got it.

Appropriately, the first manifestation of Marshall's psychic presence occurred on the day his monument was dedicated, Discovery Day, 1890. Witnesses discovered more than the magnificent monument. Witnesses said they could see the shadow of a man at the base of the pedestal although there was no object nearby that could have cast such a shadow. This is especially puzzling since the monument is on the crest of a small hill and somewhat isolated.

The elusive shadow, in the form of a man, moving from our world to the next, is not at all concerned with sun movement or proper explainable times for appearing. It has been seen at all times of the day and early evening, different times of the month and year, and through all types of weather, making it impossible to chart a pattern for its appearances. It usually starts up top, at the figure on the monument, then moves to the side of the statue and down to the dirt and disappears.

Sometimes it does not dissipate, and the shadow of the invisible man continues to be seen loitering around the imposing statue for long periods of time. Sometimes it circles the monument, and sometimes it glides down the small path toward the parking lot. Sometimes it reaches the ground and just lingers there until it fades away, and sometimes it rises again to the figure at the top, and disappears. Perhaps it is Marshall's dream, that for centuries to come, the image of his shadow shall continue to point toward the location of his discovery. He perhaps has seen it was his miraculous discovery that changed California from a land of Dons living on Spanish grants, to the populous, widely diversified state that it is today.

Gravesite of James Marshall. A mysterous shadow of a man appears. Does James Marshall refuse to rest in his grave of many years?

2.

<u>COLOMA</u>
The Gift of Gold and Ghosts

The town of Coloma goes through and beyond the State Park. The terrain continues to encompass the breathtaking American River, and share the same haunted history as the ghosts you have read about inside the park. An immense area of land gave of it's goods to make or break the hopeful miners, expanding up hills, through streams, and over vast amount of land. Other unique ghosts of the Coloma/Lotus area, yet not in the park are represented here. They tantalize, they tease, and they taunt you to engage in their activities. One such place is the Vineyard House.

<u>THE</u> <u>VINEYARD</u> <u>HOUSE</u>
Vastly Visible Voyagers

Leaving the park, there are some tantalizing tales of hauntings, with enough credibility to know imagination is not playing a part in the stories. Between owners, the Vineyard house lay vacant. It was dark and dismal, sometimes for long periods of time. Then, someone would lease or purchase the building and it would be lit with history once more. Then, again, between residents, dull, dark, and spooky.

It was during two of these recent times that folks have witnessed strange occurrences or experiences within the building. One woman, driving up the hill along the road which runs in front of the Mansion, noticed a light on in the upstairs bedroom. She knew the house had been vacant and boarded up for some time. There, looking out the window, was a woman. The driver looked at her daughter sitting beside her. "I am going to go back and see". She turned her car around only to find the building dark. Another similar incident involves people going to an evening performance at the Old Coloma Theatre just below the Vineyard House. They also saw lights flick on inside the house. Knowing the building was roped off and unoccupied, they had the presence to notify law enforcement. When the authorities arrived, their investigation proved the building to still be padlocked from the outside. No indication of entry could be found. Someone with a key was summoned, and opened the door. The building was dark, and no one was inside.

Contrary to some beliefs, most apparitions are not associated with cemeteries. Would you want to stay at your final experience at life? Ghosts may be earthbound entities, earth memory akashic images, animated astral body shells, spectral thought forms or whatever. They seldom display any interest in their decomposing physical bodies or their ashes in urns.

Ghosts are more likely to haunt the places they knew in physical life. These are usually dwellings, but sometimes they appear in hotels, pubs, office buildings, factories, or aboard ships, cockpits or galleys of airliners, roadsides, and waterways. Sometimes we can understand why they reside where they do. Others are eerie reports beyond our understanding.

There is no doubt that the Vineyard House, Coloma's historic century-old hotel is haunted. It is so proclaimed in literature distributed to tourists. Histories of the town where the gold rush began give us the details. The tragic story of this inn with a colorful past and a paranormal present has been told on such popular television programs as "It's Incredible" and "Bob Ripley's Believe It Or Not."

Today it is, unfortunately for the outside world, a private dwelling, but good news is just around the corner. The new owners are restoring this incredible mansion to its old glory. It will thankfully soon be open as an inn and restaurant again. People will flock there, as in the past. Speaking of the time before the new owners took over, guests who dined there or rented a room often witnessed one or more of the many of apparitions. For those who did, they will remain a fascinating topic for thrilling conversations for the rest of their lives.

The Vineyard rests on a hill overlooking the town. It is a four-story structure, with nineteen rooms, nine fireplaces, encircled by a porch with a second-floor balcony. The style is Victorian. The interior contains a large ballroom.

It was built in 1878-79, erected to withstand the many years to come, sturdy and solid. As has been said,"They really knew how to build them in earlier times."

But the story of the Vineyard began years before there was an inn. It is the story of two men whose lives became strangely entwined and who both experienced deplorable deaths. It is the story of Louise, the woman whom they both loved. It is the interplay of lives, both happy and tragic. Martin

22

Allhoff, a native of Germany, and Robert
Chalmers, a Scotsman, came to California
during the rush of goldseekers hoping to
make a strike in the fields of Coloma.
Mildly successful, they found some hard
earned gold but acquired no great wealth.
They both worked at odd jobs to supplement
their findings, with the hopes of traveling
back east.

Time does not tell us if they traveled
together or separately, but they both exited
California for Ohio in 1852. While back in
the Buckeye State, Allhoff married Louise
Wever, a fourteen-year-old girl. He then
brought his bride across the country, and
back to Coloma. Chalmers returned with a
wife also, plus two sons, Hugh and Abraham.

Disillusioned, and unable to make a
substantial find, both sought to end their
days in the gold fields. The difficulties
of gold mining, bloody hands, broken bones
and beaten bodies were not for them.
Especially for meager rewards. The two men
decided to engage in other occupations.
Allhoff became a vintner. He purchased a
small portion of land that he later added
to. He eventually totaled 160 acres, plenty
of room for grapes. He lost no time in
planting his vineyards and beginning his
production of wines. At harvest time the
grapes were most likely crushed in the old
world custom of dancing bare feet. The
winery became one of the finest and most
recognized in the state.

Chalmers' dream was to become an
innkeeper. He worked at various hotels until
he had learned the business, then put his
talents to work in a building called the
Sierra Nevada House. This was to be as
unique a hotel in all the gold country.

Meanwhile, Allhoff was living a joyous
life. He looked forward to many years of
prosperity with his loving wife and family.

History tells us he oversaw his vineyards with pride and accomplishment. So many rows of beautiful green vines, bearing the best varieties of grapes, Concord, Cataawha and Eden. They glistened in white and purple in the sunlight, and draped in iridescent raindrops, before harvest. Acre after acre. Beyond the vineyards were his wine cellars where the grape juices would be aged into multi-tasting delicacies. He considered himself an excellent business man. He had even struggled to put aside enough money to add additional properties for which he was negotiating. Being on top of his game, what more could a man desire?

And then the bomb fell.

His sales representative in Virginia City was arrested for tax evasion. Hearing this news, he hurried to the city. The Comstock Lode, in the heart of Nevada, Allhoff was placed under arrest for alleged tax and liquor license violations. Pending arraignment, he was ordered to remain in the city.

Mary Edity Crosley in her booklet, COLOMA: California's Golden Beginning , writes the offense wasn't considered a serious one at this time of confusion in regulations and law enforcement. "He began to worry about being sent to prison and the shame and disgrace such an event would bring to his beloved family. Night and day he brooded until the idea became an obsession...."

Finally his depression reached an endless abyss and he could no longer stand the pain. One morning as dawn was beginning to light the eastern sky, he took his tortured body to an outhouse and committed suicide. His body was brought back to Coloma and buried in what is now the Old Coloma Cemetery within sight of his home. From here he can still see the vineyards he had loved so well.

At the same time Robert Chalmers was on the road to becoming a real pillar of the community, and a serious paragon of virtue. When he acquired the Sierra Nevada Hotel, he made a decision that was unique and courageous for the gold rush country. Guests at his inn would be limited to teetotalers. Certainly not a popular stance, it would be a haven for the sober seeking refugee from the rowdy barflies outside. All this in a region indented with saloons and hotel bars, his establishment fit in like a tutu on Rambo.

At first Chalmers, expecting the best, waited in the lobby for his first customers. Hope was alight in his brown eyes. Once in a while a pie-eyed drunk who could not believe the sign out front, would stagger in the entrance. Chalmers took great pride in quickly propelling them through the egress with stern words, threateningly spoken, that, in effect, instructed the intruders to get lost and not to come back.

So, figuring the righteous would come to him, he waited and waited. And then he waited. And waited some more. Enlightenment came as he walked night after night through vacant rooms. He was forced to glance into his empty cash drawer. The lesson would be learned years later by the United States Government. Prohibition will never be popular with the general American public.

Luckily for Chalmers he did in time develop a small clientele. For the most part they consisted of the religious few who did not believe in alcohol consumption. He also housed families seeking to protect their children from the influence of the dens of iniquity all around them, of the incoming missionaries seeking to save the souls of depraved inhabitants, and of sensitive mortals from a more cultured environment who

25

felt repelled or out of place in this noisy, rowdy and rough environment of the area. Chalmers sponsored several civic affairs at his establishment as well, but though they brought many people to visit his hotel, little money crossed the threshold from this endeavor.

He soon realized he needed to look for more profitable worlds to conquer. He thought of the vast vineyards of his deceased friend, Martin Allhoff. Of course! The widow, Louise Allhoff had inherited the vineyards, winery, and cellars as well as all the other assets of her late husband. She had recently seen that all the back taxes were paid. Chalmers had always admired Louise Allhoff at a respectful distance. After all, she was the wife of a friend. He remembered her beautiful dark hair parted in the center, her blue grey eyes looking out quizzically at the world, and her dignified, majestic bearing. He was twice a widower, a free man, and she would fit perfectly into his lifes plan. He immediately lost interest in his Sierra Nevada Hotel, as he began to court the lovely Louise.

Lonely, Louise welcomed his advances. He was warm and charming, and in her eyes, handsome. When he asked for her hand in marriage she accepted. The year of 1869 was the beginning of their period of prosperity. Under Chalmers direction, more acreage was added to the vineyards, and he improved the winery until it became well known as one of the finest in the state. As with those of Allhoff before him, Chalmers wines won prize and ribbon and trophy after prize and ribbon and trophy. At the State Fair he won special awards for excellence.

His friend Allhoff had built two wine cellars, one in 1860 and the other in 1866. Chalmers added a third in 1875 with a celebration attended by the Governor of

California as well as other notables. (All the cellars contained in this stone building are now owned by the state and preserved as a historical landmark. James W. Marshall came from his cabin home and placed signed personal papers in the cornerstone. Added to this time capsule were sample bottles of wine, newspapers and other articles.)

In 1878, nine years after his marriage to Louise, Robert Chalmers began his dream home. It would be called the Vineyard House. It became the home for his family, and a hotel, considered the finest in all of Northern California. On April 4,1879, a grand opening was held, and in all its pageantry, a large crowd partied and participated in the festivities.

Then came the happy days. The Vineyard was the scene of many of the popular social activities in the area. It was the meeting place of the elite, those who had found riches and wealth in the gold fields, and those who had it without the hardships and labor. Happiness abound, and waves of laughter echoed throughout the building. Gaiety reigned. In the ballroom lucky ladies, in their best ball gowns and jewelry, danced with men groomed and in their Sunday best. The bar flowed with drinks and stories. It was the most enjoyable period in the Chalmers marriage.

The couple was thrilled to entertain a special guest during this time, ex-President Ulysses S.Grant, who answered questions about the Civil War and his administration. Timing being everything, Chalmers used the occasion to announce that he had been elected to the State Legislature. He was to serve only one term.

And then the bad times.

Unlike Allhoff, they did not start with a bomb. No, it was a creeping, insidious menace as relentless as a burglar in a high class New York neighborhood. Only this one was unstoppable. It began with Chalmers' loss of memory. Louise, of course, was the first to notice the change in her husband. Soon he was making meaningless statements, or stopping mid-sentence. He acted strangely, saying one thing and doing another. He became short of temper, frightening his wife and children, as well as the household staff. Perhaps subconsciously, he realized he was entering a realm of madness and longed for death. He would watch for a grave to be dug in the cemetery across the road. He would then lie in it, his arms crossed over his chest in the traditional position. His family and staff would have to bring him back to his mansion.

Several servants threatened to quit, and frightened for everyone's safety, Louise had a cell with iron bars constructed in the basement. She coaxingly convinced her husband he should look inside, and once there, locked the door behind him. Here, alone, in the solitary world of his own demented illness, Chalmers drifted into the crazy darkness that he was destined for, without a worry of harming others. He withered and moaned, cried out and banged his head against the bars which held him captive. Eventually he lost his eyesight and mumbled incoherently, as he moved about in this black, miserable cell. Possibly no cell was needed now, but he was still held captive as a precaution. He was fed and checked on daily, a chore no one in the family looked forward to.

Toward the end he accused his wife of trying to poison him. He refused the food they left, and literally starved. In 1881 a friend and savior arrived. It was called death. It has been suggested that Chalmers suffered from the final stages of syphilis.

Considering his conventional character and proud morality, this would not seem the case. Historians now believe his affliction might be diagnosed as Alzheimer's disease. Alzheimer's disease is an extreme form of senility, that attacks the central nervous system, thus causing disorientation and then degeneration. The symptoms would certainly fit Robert Chalmers illness.

For Louise, the death of her husband was probably a relief. She managed the vineyards well, having learned from both her husbands. The Vineyard House continued to be the most popular scene for the town's social activities. She was delighted as she prepared for what was to become the greatest day in the hotel's history.

Discovery Day in 1890. On this day as already reported, the monument to the memory of James W. Marshall was dedicated. Marshall, who died a lonely pauper five years earlier, was at last being honored. His life-size bronze statue would be atop the high pedestal over his grave. Coloma awaited the important people in government and the arts who would wine and dine at this important event.

Final touches were completed on a wing built to house the overflow. The governor, notables, and two thousand guests were served a banquet type ten course dinner under the direction of Louise Chalmers. She had hired most of the community's residents and even some of the guests, who doubled as cooks, waitresses and waiters. It was written about as a day to be remembered.

Unfortunately another bomb!

Unexpectedly, creditors appeared to harass the widow. She did not know a bank in Stockton held a substantial loan on the property. A son from Chalmers' first marriage, hearing of his death, demanded his share of the estate. He filed a civil suit against the widow. Soon she learned of other legitimate claims. Unless she could come up with an answer, Louise and her children, two by Allhoff and a daughter by Chalmers, might lose everything they had worked for. Stressed, she silently wished for another husband to take care of her and the children as Allhoff and then Chalmers had done in the past. This would be as patterns before, her saving grace. Unfortunately, this did not happen. Older now, she did not have the trimmings to trap another husband that quickly. Especially fast enough to save her empire. It must be said, the gal stuck with it, in and out of the courts, giving the good fight.

After three years of litigation, a judge deeded her the hotel and ten acres of land. Without the money to afford proper care, the vineyards and winery experienced disaster. With threat of racial discrimination, Chinese workmen she had employed fled for their safety. No longer able to employ guards, the vines were ravaged by animals, both human and critters. A blight killed the surviving plants. As the crops withered the winery processing buildings fell into disrepair. She realized it was hopeless and gave up the fight. She and her brood were still living quite comfortably inside her distinguished mansion, and she longed to find a way she could stay there for the remainder of her life.

The bank took pity on her. They foreclosed, but allowed Louise to remain on a rent paying basis. To meet her monthly payments she reduced room rents in order to keep them occupied. She soon signed a deal to allow the basement, indeed her husbands damp cell, to be used as the town jail. In due time, she signed over her remaining property rights to pay her attorney.

When her lawyer died a short time later,

his heirs sold the property to Martin Allhoff, Jr., and his partner. Thus a part of the property originally acquired by a father came to a son. Martin gave his mother full reign as she continued to run her beloved Vineyard House. But, seeing no need for them, he dismantled most of the other buildings. The wine cellars were spared, and later sold to the State of California for permanent preservation. Louise died in 1900, taking her memories, good and bad, with her to her grave across the street.

But strange occurrences had been happening. Robert Chalmers, although dead, refused to leave his mansion. Some part of his psyche, a spirit choosing to be earthbound or perhaps in the form of an etheric double with biological memories, was stubbornly determined to remain at the Vineyard House. Tenants now complained of mysterious voices and sounds, of ghostly footsteps and stompings, echoing along the corridors in what should have been the quiet hours of darkness. One boarder fled in the middle of the night so frightened he refused to say what he had seen.

For many decades the Vineyard was operated as a run-down rooming house and restaurant under a succession of owners. Ghost rumors abounded and the weird phenomena continued. Guests continued to complain of hearing the rustling of skirts, metalic clangs and heavy breathing. It seems paranormal effects from one source can attract manifestations from other origins in a general psychic atmosphere.

One couple from Sacramento said they heard a group of noisy guests to the Vineyard House enter the front door and start up the stairs. Planning to complain, they opened their door to quiet the revelers. What they saw were three men in Victorian clothing. They vanished before their eyes.

The serious resurrection of the Vineyard began in 1975 when Gary Herrera, a former Oakland restauranteur, purchased the property in partnership with his brother and sister-in-law, Frank and Darlene Herrera, and friend, David Van Buskirk.

With impeccable taste, they went to work on a labor of love. Floors, stairs and balustrades were stripped to the natural wood. Walls were papered. Paint was applied where needed, which meant everywhere. They found forgotten furniture in the dark corners of the attic. They refurbished, the plan being to bring the mansion back to it's original glory.

"I thought I knew what I was getting into when I purchased the Vineyard House," a cordial Gary Herrera told the author. "I thought the house would be perfect for a restaurant and inn, and was anxious to put my plan into effect. There were many hours of hard work, reconstruction and modification before we could open for business. And, besides the years of neglect and age, having to fight to bring the building up to code, there seemed to be something beyond our control working against us."

No matter what plans Gary made for redecorating, it seemed to be predestined. "I would painstakingly choose colors and fabrics, ordering vibrant shades for bedspreads, curtains, wallpaper, paint and accessories," Gary remembered. "My order would arrive in completely contrasting shades than what I had asked for. This was to happen consistently. Imagine my surprise when thumbing through an old Vineyard scrapbook. The colors and fabrics that had been delivered matched the original Vineyard House decor." Gary was happy to show us the goose bumps on his arms. "I began to realize somebody from beyond our world wanted to keep this house the way it was.

"Actually, strange things began to happen right after I purchased the mansion," said Gary in retrospect. "A cup would be misplaced, a treasured bud vase would disappear and be rediscovered in some ungodly and most unlikely spot. We all joked about 'gremlins,' but inwardly we shrugged it off as absent-mindedness, because we were so busy. I chastised myself for being so careless. The more carefully I checked my every action, the more I realized it wasn't me. It was, and is, something beyond my world of understanding!"

"Same here" Frank Herrera, a partner and a man not given to believing in the supernatural. "My logical mind tried to come up with any understandable reason for the strange occurrences. I was reluctant to discuss with the others such things as curtains blowing when the windows were closed, and cold drafts when I walked down otherwise warm corridors. Now I don't look for an explanation for these things," Frank said, thoughtfully. "But it doesn't take those 'cold pockets' to give me the chills. I had shivers already."

David Van Buskirt, Gary's other partner was startled to find several old style wood coffins under the porch during the restoration. It was known that several prisoners who occupied the basement jail in the 1800's had been executed, strung from an old oak tree in the front yard of the Vineyard House. Just as hasty burials followed in the cemetery across the street. The owners found another old fashion wood coffin in an old crawl space when remodeling the basement. More goose bumps! Apparently they kept a stack available for future occupants.

Today Robert Chalmers' ghost bangs the

33

walls when he is aggravated. His spirit takes pride in annoying the guests that do not meet with his approval. His presence is felt throughout the house, including the basement, which when occupied houses a downstairs dungeon-like pub, alongside the cell he once occupied. In life he was not a man sympathetic to the act of drinking alcohol. A shame, it might have eased his pain in his final hours. Too late now. Chalmer's spirit, unchanged since life, is especially critical of the activity surrounding the bar at the Vineyard House.

"One night while tending bar in the downstairs pub," Frank was to recall, "my customers and I were startled to see one cup in a series of eight hanging from nails on the wall begin to rattle by itself. "It tweaked and moved while the others were still. "A hollow silence ensued," he said, "we were engrossed in watching the spectacle." Then, the cups banged and bumped against the others in random disorder. "Soon after, the cups calmed and the clanging subsided as suddenly as it began. I wanted to believe another freakish incident was over," Frank said.

Not so!

A customer ready to resume his drinking, and after seeing the previous event, asked for a straight shot of whiskey to calm his nerves. "I was happy to oblige," said Frank, "and perhaps have one myself! I picked up dual shot glasses from beneath the counter, and wrists up, placed them together on the bar. I turned momentarily to grab the bottle who's liquid would fill the glasses. As I turned back, ready to pour, I saw the teetering and jumping of those two shot glasses, unaided by human hands, proceed to slide across the bar to the waiting customer. Empty!"

The customer pulled his chair away from

the bar. "He decided he didn't want another drink after all," said Frank, remembering. "If we have a ghost, he is a thoughtful one. The ghost figured the customer had enough to drink for one night. It was one of those rambunctious moods for our wayward spirit," he recalled. "And, I was ready to close the bar for the night anyway!"

"I saw a ghost at the Vineyard House," a resident of the area told us. "My girlfriend and I had gone upstairs to look at the bedrooms which had recently been redecorated. She went to look out the window, and after she had turned her back to me, I switched the light out to scare her. Right then I heard the springs give as if someone sat down on one of the beds. I thought it was my girlfriend and that my joke hadn't worked, so I turned the light back on. In front of us, sitting on the bed, was the figure of a man with a beard." His voice lowered. "The man stared sternly at us as if he didn't like the idea that we were in the bedroom. All of a sudden he began to fade, and we ran down the stairs." The man thought about the situation. My guess is that it was Robert Chalmers we saw. There is a picture hanging on the wall in the living room of the Vineyard house, and the guy sure looked like him. And it was his bedroom that we were in!"

Other guests to the Vineyard House have heard the calling of wild birds in the hallway between the upstairs bedrooms. Overnight guests have often complained of someone trying to turn their locked doorknobs after they have retired for the night, or to awaken in the morning with their bedroom door wide open. Invisible children run in the halls and play with their toys in front of the upstairs bedrooms.

"I was a housekeeper for the Vineyard House," a former employee told Gold Rush Ghosts. "One day while I was alone in the house, the phone rang. I was working in one of the bedrooms, so I put down my dust rag and went down the hall to answer it. I couldn't have been gone more than a minute, but when I returned to the bedroom, there was an indentation on the bedspread that I had just made. The mark indicated someone had laid down on the bed, because it was definitely an outline of a reclining body." She smiled a knowing smile. "Someone had laid on the newly made bed. I got the heck out of there and it was a long time before they could convince me to work in the place alone!"

On the other hand, some people were 'dying' to get hired on. "Think of the adventure in it" one hopeful said. Other employees at the Vineyard House got used to ghostly pranks. "I was once locked in the upstairs ladies' restroom for over an hour," one of the hired help told us. "I had to wait until someone came along to unlock the door from the outside."

Tom Christopherson, another former employee of the Vineyard House told the author in 1998, "I once had the radio on, and all by itself the station changed from a rock station to mariachi music." Other unexplainable things became commonplace. "Coffee pots often turned themselves on" Christopherson said. "I remember one night being in the building alone after we had closed, and sat down in one of the banquet rooms to have a piece of cake before closing up. I instantly felt invisible people watching me. I decided to forget about the cake!"

The community seems to accept the Vineyard House as being haunted. There are a few that wouldn't set foot in the place if

36

you paid them, but the majority of the customers enjoy the spooky atmosphere along with the good food and accommodations, when it is open. The Vineyard House is a fascinating combination of a colorful past that continues to survive while looking very much the same as it did in the 1800s. Right down to the spirits who lived back then and are still around.

The last time Gold Rush Ghosts was inside this beautiful Vineyard House a fire was burning in the Franklin stove in the dining room. The tables were displayed in brown and white checkered cloths centered with kerosene lamps. Much of the chinaware was original to the house. Other plates and silverware were contributed by older Coloma residents. Patterns therefor varied making it so very homey. Upstairs, every bedroom was different. Each room was named after a famous person from the Gold Rush era, many who had stayed there. There is the Lola Montez suite, and the Lottie Crabtree bedroom. Some had brass bedsteads, others had huge Victorian foot and headboards. Perhaps Robert Chalmers already knows how his Vineyard House has been reborn, as he and his phantom guests roam proudly about his creation. And Louise, she seems to want to stay as well. We hope they are both happy.

The Vineyard House will soon be open to the public again, but for now we ask that you respect the new owners privacy. It is a beautiful house and easily seen from the road or the pioneer cemetery across the street. It is a wonderful piece of gold rush history with mysteries still unlocked.

OKEI-
A Lonely Spirit Wants To Go Home

The Chinese were not the only orientals to come to Coloma. The Japanese also migrated to the Mother Lode. A federal census shows there were only 55 Japanese in the United States in 1870. Of this number 33 made their homes in California. Of these, twenty-two Japanese settlers were located in Gold Hill, the area southwest of Coloma. The first of these immigrants from Japan arrived in June of 1869 under the leadership of a noble German soldier of fortune, John Henry Schnell, a follower of the Lost Aizu Wakamatsu. It is believed the colony started as a refuge for the ruling family, brought upon by the downfall of the Tokugawa Shogunate. They may have been forced to flee their motherland but they brought with them their history, in the form of tea plants, bamboo roots, seeds, silk cocoons, and as many of the other important products of their culture that they could carry. They had hopes of establishing themselves in the new land. And so it was arranged by a family called Schell, for Okei, a beautiful young Japanese girl, to come to America and serve as their nursemaid.

About a year later, the Japanese colony knew it was in trouble. Scorching summer heat, poor soil, and the changing of the direction of upstream water by gold miners, made their chances for survival in this new land almost impossible. Financial help promised from their motherland never arrived, and the colonists were forced to disband. Many returned to Japan. Only two remained in the Coloma area, a man called Matsunosuke Sakuri and the beautiful Okei, the young nursemaid. Both were happy to secure employment with one of Coloma's pioneer families. Sakurai, seemingly happy, worked in the community until his death on February 25, 1901. His body was interred in the local Vineyard House (Pioneer) Cemetery. Having enough of this world as far as we know, his death apparently put his spirit to rest.

Okei was not as lucky. Legend tells us she longed for her homeland. In a country unfamiliar to her, she was lonely. She would often climb up a hill near the Schell household to be alone. She would look off into the horizon as if she could see her birthplace.....Japan. She sickened soon after her friends disbandment of the colony, and her body withered. She died of fever, probably caused by her weakened condition. Knowing how much she loved it, Okei was buried on her beloved knoll, to forever face the motherland she spent her days dreaming about. After the burial she was forgotten until sixty-eight years ago, when the gravesite was accidently rediscovered.

On this very knoll, in the center of what is now a cow pasture, stands a lone tombstone, old and worn. It reads:

In Memory of
OKEI
Died 1871
Aged 18 years
A Japanese Girl

The grave became a historical monument, as prior to World War II, groups of Japanese people visited the site. It is now on private property.

To those who do not believe, they are all gone now. How unimaginative. Our research shows otherwise. The miners, the saloon keepers, gamblers, the ladies of the night, have certainly all been dust for many years. Today Coloma lies almost untouched by time on a gentle curve of the slow-flowing South Fork of the American River. The tiny town of many ghosts rolls up its imaginary sidewalks sometime around October 1 each year. The townsfolk casually sigh with relief as they waits out another mild winter. On the first of April, the travelers begin to flock once again to this seasonal tourist town. Coloma is primarily supported by the rafting trade. History buffs, vacationers, and gold panners also come, the miners with hopes as those of the past, to find that great nugget. Many explore, examine and marvel at this hypnotic place that changed the course of history. Last year Coloma suffered through heavy storms, and many come with hopes of gold being washed down from the hills. Today, if the old buildings were not there, one could never believe that this sleepy, peaceful, out-of-the-way community of few residents, once inhabited masses of people in its town and surrounding hills. Minus the miners, Coloma is remarkably the same as it was in the 1800's. Many of the old buildings and historic sites of the gold-rush era are preserved and remain intact, the same as the legends and stories that accompany them. Eerie age-old sun dried bits of miners' skeletons, rusty gold pans, and personal possessions such as coins and watches are still found in the hills and streams. From this we are continuously reminded that the search for gold was a violent, turbulent one. It is no wonder that ghosts and spirits of these unfortunates abound, those with dreams of gold, those that luck had run out on as they met bullets, hangman's ropes and excruciating pain in their last hours on earth. They still choose to surround the hills, sneer at those at the waterways, and stay close to the old buildings of long ago. Perhaps they still feel they can stake a claim. Perhaps, in a strange way, the gold rush country is their claim, for all time. Coloma is described as serene but spooky, even by the last remaining die-hards that "Just don't believe in ghosts."

3.

HAUNTED HIGHWAYS
Harrowing Highway Experiences

There are roads that cross all over our country. Some through the vast expanse of deserts. Some wind through mountains, and pass through shaded forests. Some cross over rivers, and some follow ancient Indian trails. Some of these lead to abandoned farmhouses and sagging barns where once people with dreams were born, lived and loved. They are all gone now, leaving the remnants of their lives to rot and rust.

We remember the highways that parallel the routes of the pioneers....the 49ers, the Overland, the Oregon Trails. In some places one can take a short walk from the paved roads, and see the ruts left by the wagon wheels on their dirty and hard westerly treks to the distant promised land of California.

There are places along streets and roads that are called "haunted" or "magnetic". It is here you may want to stop your vehicle, turn off it's motor, put the gears in neutral and release the brakes. The car will appear to roll uphill. These are optical illusions, so curious they are almost impossible to be believed. You have no spooks here, folks!

But there are, to be certain, vast stretches of road that are known to be haunted. Sometimes they are active during

42

the daylight hours, but more frequently at night. The specter of a human or animal will appear out of nowhere, in the direct path of your car. As a motorist you veer off into a ditch or hit a tree. The apparition vanishes. Sometimes the road is straight ahead and free of known obstructions, but still the accidents occur. Law enforcement officers know where they are. They are used to them because of the frequency of accidents.

Anything can occur. There are many types of strange phenomena. One is the stoppage of automotive engines without apparent cause. You will remember the oft repeated story of the girl waving in the road that the motorists picks up. He takes her to her home and she disappears at the front door. When the girls mother answers the door she tells the motorist her daughter is dead. She was buried in the exact clothes she was wearing when the driver picked her up. Oriental philosophers believe these visions to be Akashic Records, or the earth memory. Perhaps it is so.

PROSPECTOR ROAD
The Old Way To Coloma

The winding hillside known as Prospector Road is considered one of the most haunted roads in the Gold Rush country. It's pavement runs over old mines, old claims, and the bodies that lived it's history. In some cases, the collapse of tunnels gave miners premature burials, some died as a result of being eliminated by other greedy miners.

Prospector Road is in some places little more than a one lane path, as it runs the seven mile stretch adjacent to the convenient and more traveled county built Marshall Road. If you're in a hurry, it's Marshall that you want. Another plus and to be remembered, the county is responsible for maintaining Marshall Road. It's primary function when constructed in 1957, was to accommodate the ever increasing traffic to the area. The road diligently follows the hazardous cliff from Lotus to Georgetown. If you are looking for ghosts, however, and have the time to spend, Prospector, (Often called the "Old Road"), is what you are looking for. It was built by Chinese labor in the 1800's, and cuts the winding mountainside connecting with Marshall at both Lotus and Garden Valley. The barely traveled road and surrounding terrain has a colorful Gold Rush history. It is well documented the treacherous nature of the countryside caused many a wagon, and later automobile, to overturn, spilling their passengers down the hillside to their painful date with death. An old stagecoach stop, since moved from it's original site, is still visible on private acreage along Prospector Road. It was built as a half-way mark between Lotus and Garden Valley for the comfort of weary travelers. Later a line shack and check station was built along Prospector for the O'Brien and Maxwell Cromite Mines, both prosperous businesses, cromite being a needed commodity during World War I for ammunition. But back to the Gold Rush days.

In the 1800's, substantial gold discoveries were made in these hills, which account for its name. As with the age-old stories of prospecting and claim jumping, many a foolish miner who bragged a bit too openly about his "find" was coincidentally lost among the hills of Prospector. Their bodies were often never recovered, and more

44

often never looked for. It is known that many spirits roam the Prospector hills, and at least one is still seeking the gold he never recovered while having his life cut short while trying.

Perhaps it was his specter who frightened a young couple with poltergeist-like pranks after they settled in a new home along the Road.

It was late one night the pretty young bride awakened from her fretful slumber. She was cold and had a feeling of something amiss. She pulled the covers up. Then she remembered making a large log fire before retiring, one that should have kept the house warm till morning. She turned her head to see the reflection on the wall, observing the wood still burning in the stove. She was grateful for the mirror on the wall which made this possible from her second story bedroom. Then her imagination kicked in, and she thought she heard unnatural noises in the house. She carefully and gently woke her husband, who was not to thrilled to be getting out of bed to indulge her. Together they went down the stairs.

"I knew my husband had locked and bolted the front door before we went to bed" she told us. "Now it was ajar. The bolt pin was still in the outward position, yet the wall slot where it should still be secured had not been torn." The couple could find no evidence of forced entry.

The mystery of the unexplained open door went unanswered. Everything else appeared as it should. That is, except for their dog. Hearing a frightened whimper, they turned to find their pet huddled and trembling in a corner of the room. Consoling the animal, the husband opened the door and looked outside into the darkness. Nothing! He carefully went around the house. Nope! Thus the family was introduced to the ghost of

Prospector Road.

He is a wily old cuss. This apparition is described by residents as rugged, big, stocky and attired in old pants, or work like clothes. Sometimes he has a canvas looking rain coat pulled over his head. To those who are able to see him, he appears semi-transparent, tall and craggy. Some say he is sporting a beard. To those who cannot see him, but endor his wrath, he is considered a pesky, annoying trickster. The legend goes, and most folks believe, his purpose is to keep people away from a claim he never recovered.

The young couples cabin is nicely hidden in the underbrush, barely visible from the road. They moved here because they thought it would be a great place to let their dog run, and to have a family grow up. After a year of the dog refusing to take advantage of his new found privilege, they retired back to the city. Bowser is happy once again, and though ten years have passed since the incident, and age and knowledge is certainly a factor now, this faithful companion has not changed his mind about Prospector. "We went back a few months ago to see the old place, but Bowser would not get out of the car. He shivered until we were back on the freeway. He's 110 lbs, and wanted to sit in my lap in the front seat!"

People complain that tall field grass spreads when no one is walking through it on Prospector Road. Bowser is not the only dog to cower and bristle. One couple called us after they returned from hunting. "We put our guns down and fell asleep. The rifles were still loaded and on the kitchen table because we thought we would give it one more try later in the day. When we awoke the bullets were next to the gun." There is also the story of children being locked in their bedroom from the outside. The door sported one of those old fashioned locks, and the key, if it ever did exist, was lost many many years ago, through a series of owners and renters. The father had to remove the door to free his children. People who live in the homes along Prospector Road talk of items being moved, and strange noises. It is a known fact that things are different on Prospector Road. Those who live or continuously play here, and have seen the ghost of the miner, feel less frightened or threatened than those who encounter him when traveling through.

Billy, (now known as Bill) had his first ghostly encounter over ten years ago as a teenager, and although he has since moved away and started his own family, he remembers as if yesterday. His Mother and Dad still live in the same place on Prospector Road, and he admits to hoping that someday his own children will encounter the ghost. They have long heard the story, both from their dad and their Grandma and Grandpa.

"We had decided to take a walk" Bill said, speaking of his boyhood friends. "My folks were entertaining, and it was boring. A beautiful night, we entertained ourselves by pushing each other into the bushes, and talking about school and girls. We rounded a curve in the path and all stopped. Fear engulfed us in such a way we became transfixed in time. We could not move. There in the moonlight we saw the figure of a tall man materialize before us. He was draped in a tarp-like material which appeared to be a tattered rain garment." Bill took a deep breath, remembering. Whether the apparition heard the startled teenagers, or if he was to do so from some twisted coincidence of fate, the enraged swaying specter turned and glared fixedly at the boys.

"You cannot understand real fright until your eyes meet those of a ghost" Bill exclaimed to us, perspiration on his forehead. "We didn't know whether to run or stand still so that it wouldn't come after us. My biggest fear at that time was that it would touch me."

The boys stood still as living tombstones as the apparition pointed a finger at them accusingly. Later upon separate interrogation, each boy was to confirm the same description and order of events. From Bill's own words, "It appeared his feet were not standing on the ground, but maybe a foot above. He swayed lightly from side to side. We couldn't really see through him, but there seemed to be transparencies around his frame. He looked cold and wet, bluish in color, though the evening was hot, at least 85 degrees, and dry. We had not seen rain in months. With his finger still pointed directly at us, the ghost opened his mouth to say something we could not hear. He slowly, deliberately mouthed soundless words we could not understand."

The boys then broke from their transfixed state, and raced for Bill's house. Perhaps this broke the "spell", or perhaps because it was simply time, the unearthly vision turned, and floated down the embankment.

After hearing the story, Bill and his buddies escorted their parents to the spot where they had seen the ghost but he had vanished. There were no footprints, broken twigs, nothing! Upset, it took the adults several hours to calm the boys.

The fright of the boys was doubtlessly genuine. Bill acquired temporary psychological problems. At the insistence of their parents, all of the boys went through counseling. Never did one of them deviate from their stories of the ghost and how they had observed him.

"I also saw the miner, and it is quite common" Carmon Fredricks told the author in the summer of 1997. He took the author to the same spot where Bill had his experience. "I saw him as clearly as I am looking at you" he said. "Only difference, he faded away. I don't suspect you will do that" he smiled. People in the area call him the "Old Prospector" and people who live around here figure he is buried under that ground."

Bills dad has his own stories to tell.

"We had a shop in an old out-building on the property. Along the walls were hooks and shelves I had put together to hold my tools. Things were usually in order unless I was building something."

"Anyway, one day we had made a commitment to help some friends who's car was broke down. Bill, my friend Dave, and I took some tools off the shelf, all the things we would need in this endeavor, and packed them into my truck. We went back several times to be sure we had everything before I covered the tools with a tarp, and off we went.

"When we got to our destination we took the tarp off and there were no tools. The only thing I could think of was that they had to have been stolen when we stopped for a burger. It seemed unlikely that anyone could have known what was under the cover, much less get $400 dollars worth of tools out without disturbing the tarp in any way, but we had no other explanation. We had to go around to my friends neighbors and several trips to the store to get enough tools to complete the job.

"Luckily, I was insured," the man continued. "I filed a complaint with the Sheriff's Department and as soon as we returned home, I intended to call my insurance agent. But it wasn't necessary," he added, a look of disbelief in his eyes.

"When we returned to the shop all the tools were in their proper spaces on the shelf, as if they had never been removed. Someone, or something, still as yet unknown to this world took them out of the truck. My God, that's spooky!"

"Then again," the man said, "That damn shed has a lock that can only be hitched from the inside. The shed has no windows, and only one door. The door has a lock and a key so it can be locked from the outside too, but sometimes when I am inside, and don't want to be disturbed, I will lock it from the inside. Well, one day we found the door locked from the inside. The lock is one of those with a bar across, not one that could trip up by itself. It would definitely take someone on the inside of the building to lock it. Yet when I called out, no one answered from inside the place. When Bill got home we broke the door down, taking half the door casing with it, to get back into the shed. I made Bill wait outside, and I went into the building with a gun, thinking perhaps a vagrant had gotten into it, actually not knowing what to think. There was no one inside. Not a trace of a person! Somehow the door was locked from the inside and without a way for whomever locked it to get back outside. Isn't that impossible? It's simply impossible.! Right?" Wrong!

On a cold, blustery night about 10:30 p.m., a waitress returning from her job in Coloma drove the winding cliff on Marshall Road just above the area where the ghost had been seen on Prospector Road. The road was slick, the going slow. Wanting to get home soon as possible, she only rubbed the front windshield on the driver's side of the car clean enough of frost so that she could see to drive. The rest of the windshield remained covered with ice. As she turned the curve which placed her car just above

50

the area where the stagecoach stop rests below her, she heard a loud crash. On the passenger side of the windshield, imbedded in the frost, appeared the distinct outline of an outstretched hand and arm. She feared she must have hit someone, though the mountain road was deserted at this time of the night, certainly no person in their right mind would venture to walk it.

The driver pulled off to the side of the road, taking out a flashlight. Trembling, she got out of her car, and searched the road and embankment for a body. There was none. She looked for fallen branches, anything that could have crashed into her windshield leaving the mark. Nothing! Shaking, she got back into her car, looking at the mark on the windshield. The hand and arm did not begin to fade as it again filled with frost until she reached her home, four miles away.

That same night, at approximately the same time, a strange voice was heard outside the young couple's cabin. They had seen the waitress' car lights ascended Marshall Road just above their house and the old stagecoach stop. As the family carried a final load of firewood from their truck into their cabin, a voice was distinctly heard. It said: "Stay away from my claim."

HIGHWAY 50
A Little Boy's Guardian Angel

A three year old little boy sat silently next to his dead mother's body. Their car had veered off Highway 50, on a stretch of road beyond the lights of Placerville, and just above the smaller hamlet of Pollock Pines. A remote area, the car had plummeted down a 40 foot embankment, landing in a clump of underbrush and trees, obscuring it from view. The horrible accident occurred in June of 1994, just as this loving mother and her child were headed for an enjoyable holiday with friends in Carson City, Nevada. In a moments time, tiny Nicky Skubish's world was forever changed. He now knew the horror of being alone in a strange place both in darkness and the excruciating heat of day. He knew the horror of having a Mother so close but unable to help him. His fate would have him survive five days in sweltering heat without food or water. Luckily, sometimes at night a spirit woman would visit young Nick to console him and hold him through the night. But time was running out.

The stretch of Highway 50 that runs through the Gold Rush Country has long been known to be haunted. Stories of old miners, loggers, and mules, seen, and then disappearing along the side of the road are commonplace. There are stories of motorists who swerve to avoid hitting a tattered looking phantom, only to find the apparition gone when they look in the rear view mirror. Some experts feel the area surrounding Highway 50 is encased in a time warp, where the present overlaps yesterday on a continuous basis. It's nothing new. This is true of most of the Mother Lode.

In 1996 Cheryl Anderson of Tracy, driving on Highway 50, saw through her windshield in front of her, two men digging up the road between Placerville and Pollock Pines. She took her foot off the accelerator, thinking that any minute a 'slow down men working' sign would appear. As she got closer, the men disappeared. "It was unnerving" she was to tell the author. Nothing like this has ever happened to me. I thought I was loosing my mind!" She was grateful when Gold Rush

<u>Ghosts</u> was able to confirm that she was not the first person to voice such experiences.

But back to the boy. The local Sheriffs Department had searched the area thoroughly when the Skubish's were reported missing. In fact, a search team went over the exact spot where his mother's car had left the road, and felt certain there was no sign of an accident.

On the evening of the fourth day after the accident, a motorist on Highway 50 was amazed to see a naked woman lying alongside the road. A strange occurrence, the incident was immediately reported to the authorities. A search team was dispatched to search the area, but the naked woman was gone and nothing of suspicious nature was found. The couple reporting the incident were above reproach and a hoax was ruled out. The following morning, a lone deputy, puzzled, decided to search the area again, and this time was amazed to find a child's shoe. It had not been there the night before. Straining to see down the embankment, the wreckage soon became apparent to him. He called for back-up, and started down hill, obviously expecting the worse.

Little Nicky Skubish miraculously made a complete recovery. He insisted a woman came to see him at night. Nothing could dissuade him from his story.

Was the unknown spirit woman who visited Nicky the spirit of his dead mother, and knowing that time was running out for her son, somehow was able to materialize at the side of the road in a plea for help? And did she do so naked to further attract attention? There is no limit to a mother's love. Or, was it an angel dispatched to aid a little child.

The story was to make National headlines, and caused several television shows including "Unsolved Mysteries" to explore the options.

Still, folks around Placerville don't find it quite so unusual. And most of them don't buy the theory that little Nicky was perhaps hallucinating. And how can drivers hallucinate a naked woman lying in the road? Especially when your sober!

Hogwash! The only answer is God in whatever name or way you choose to perceive a higher being, is good and merciful and chose to protect this precious toddler. That's all we need to know.

4.

PLACERVILLE
Horrific Hangman Hauntings

In 1849 Placerville was called Hangtown, and was considered one of the major camps in the gold country. Originally known as "Old Dry Diggin's", the town's notorious and frequent hangings accounted for her name change, and the stigma still "hovers" today, in the form of disembodied spirits that haunt the town, the cemeteries, the old buildings and surrounding mountains and hills. Miners, weary of the crowds in Coloma, came looking for fertile ground in which to pan and placer mine. Old Dry Diggin's was a rich find.

Unfortunately, as news spread, Hangtown was overcome with prospectors, the ever hopefuls, and as always, the element of greed and deceit. Claim jumping, murders, and lawlessness became commonplace, and the question was no longer who to hang, but how many at a time. Justice was quick, a trial and hanging often on the same day, and sometimes for trivial offences, as patience was not a sanctity in those days. Kicking a man's dog could cost you your neck, and touching his gold could cost you 39 lashes before the hanging. Several famous men got their starts in the hills of Placerville as well. Phillip Armour started with a butcher shop to feed the miners, and J.M. Studebaker contracted to build wheelbarrows for the needy.

There were also the heros. For twelve long years, in the best and worse of weather, Snowshoe Thompson rode across the Sierra between Genoa, Carson City in Nevada, and Placerville, a long and treacherous 90 miles to insure the miners their mail, medicine, and hand held supplies. Often letters from home was the only solace for the hard working prospectors, and they looked to Snowshoe, especially when things were going poorly.

Plagued by fires, the town rebuilt and rebuilt again. Many of the old buildings still stand today, and many are haunted. Some of the old buildings are gone, but the ghosts remain. Here "lies" the stories of some of them.

THE HANGMAN'S TREE
A Drink, a Handshake, and a Ghost

Sitting on a bar stool in the spot where over 1000 hangings took place in the 1800's, might well "spook" the average person, but for the hearty customers of the Hangman's Tree Lounge, it is primarily just another reminder of a time when the town was frothed with prospectors and unfortunates. Often they hail their glasses in the air, in a silent "toast" to their fallen brothers. After all, not all those hung were guilty of a horrendous crime. Some were just put to death, in case!

Located in what is now lower Main Street, The Hangman's Tree is a very popular lounge, purchased seventeen years ago by Jim & Ruby DeCair. A bar since 1933, and considered the oldest lounge in Placerville, the history of the place, and things that go "Bump in the night" do not razzle the proprietors. "Sure we hear things we cannot explain." Ruby was to tell the author. "It's an old building. People often talk about something strange happening in the bar. I do know a night bartender we had some time ago said he saw a ghost in the building and he was not the type to tell tales." She told us. She shook her head, and then handed us an article from an old newspaper. "Here are some people that have had experiences with our ghosts."

Our investigative staff came up with newer and more startling evidence.

"It's the same guy." Stated Rosemary Dean, our well known Psychic Investigator, pointing to the wall. "Yes. I call him Willy because he gives me the willys! He stares, watches. Darn guy doesn't just walk into a room either" She added. "He floats, or appears to be wheeled around. His feet never seem to move, and I see him in the Fairchild Building down the street where I have my office, and at the Chamber of Commerce Building across the street on Main as well."

"Must be the man who had the job as the hangman." She went on, "He has a sadness about him. And, he seems to take a morbid interest in what the hanging victim feels. It's like he wonders about their pain."

The Hangman's Tree lounge sits directly over the spot of the official Hangman's Tree of the 1800's in Placerville. There are many old trees in Placerville, and most of them saw their fair share of hangings. Two, long chopped down, existed in the immediate facility of Main Street, one at the lounge, and the other above what is now the Chamber of Commerce building. Folks at the Chamber of Commerce also see the same man, as he makes his rounds from place to place. Dean has an office in the old Fairchild Building between the two. Interestingly, her office is on the second floor, and the majority of the activity at the Chamber of Commerce building is on that level too.

At the Hangman's Tree he is seen downstairs, and sometimes floating above, which would be at the height of the scaffolds. In front of the Hangman's Tree Lounge is a yellow Historic Marker, No.# 141. Once you enter the old building, you can feel the ominous, the aura of another time. As you take a seat at the bar, and embrace the friendliness of the crew, you know at once it is okay to experience the ghostly apparitions, (if you are that lucky) or to discuss it with anyone who has.

Carla Phillips, longtime resident and a total believer was eager to discuss her experience. "I came in for a beer with my husband after work" She told us. "It was a hot day last July, and we needed a break. After the second beer I needed to go to the restroom. I excused myself and headed in that direction. I saw a man coming out of the ladies room, and I thought that it was odd, but assumed the men's room must be out of order. He was dressed real funny, like, in black and with a top hat. I thought to myself, 'Maybe we were having a Pioneer's Day Parade or something.' Anyway, when I went back to my seat he was not in the bar. I asked my husband if he saw him leave, and he said no. No one else had seen him either, and there was no parade that day or anything."

Phillips assured us she had only had two beers. "I was not drunk" She stated emphatically. "If I was I could have come up with something more original than a tall man in black. I do believe this was a highlight in my life. Imagine seeing a ghost! Wow!"

Robin Elliott who has worked as a

bartender for the Hangman's Tree off and on for seventeen years, and is also a longtime resident of the area, told the author, "As a child I always heard rumors of a haunting in the building. People spoke of seeing a man, and also of things being moved around. In the 16 years I have worked here there have been some real spooky things that have happened."

The pretty brunette began to recall her encounters with the unknown. "One night when we had Christmas lights on, I was reminiscing with a bunch of customers. Just as we started talking about the ghosts, the lights on the wall in one section dimmed. They stayed that way for about 20 seconds. It was real eerie!"

"Often times when my back is turned, I feel someone watching me from behind, like at the jukebox area" She continued. "When I turn around, there is no one there. And more than once, as we get ready to close for the night I go thru the usual routine of opening the restroom doors. When I go back, they are closed again."

"I do believe the most startling thing is the shot glasses" She told us. We put them on the shelf, and find them in the ice. This is completely impossible. If they were to fall off the shelf they would hit the counter. They would have to FLY to reach the ice." Elliott also has a friend who carried on a conversation with someone at the bar, only to turn around and find there was no one there.

Just a few years ago, while working at night on the business adjacent to the Hangman's Tree, a workman was startled to see a tall man, in black, walk thru the wall from the Hangman's Tree part of the building, stand in front of him, and silently disappear. With the controlled swiftness of one in shock, the contractor came down off his ladder, walked to the counter to retrieve his keys, and leaving his tools where they lay, left the building. He did not return until the sun came out the following day. Guess babysitting ghosts was not part of his contract.

In 1849 three desperados were hung at the same time from the tree at the location of the Hangman's Tree Lounge. Rumor has it they were given 39 lashes and were close to death from the beatings. Townfolks hung them anyway. History has conflicting stories as to what their crime was, some accounts say robbery, others say cheating at cards and a nasty fight afterwards that ended in a murder. Their remains were apparently not worth the trek to boot hill, because they were buried behind the tree which is now a parking lot by Highway 50. On January 24, 1959, the James W. Marshall chapter of E. Clampus Vitus erected a monument to mark the spot. It reads,

> "Somewhere here lie the remains of the three unfortunates hanged in late 1849 from the oak tree in the feed corral. After a fair trial by the vigilantes this incident changed the name of Dry Diggin's to Hangtown. Let us not judge to harshly, for those were Rough Days of the Great Gold Rush."

Imagine the owner, Ruby De Cair's startling experience when opening the bar one crisp fall morning. "I put my key in the door and opened as I always do. As I walked through the doors to turn the light on I saw a man sitting in the table directly in front of me. He was wearing a tall hat and a black coat. I jumped, turned around, and he disappeared!"

It is easy to recognize the Hangman's Tree when you approach 305 Main Street in Placerville. Hanging from his neck from the second story of the building is 'George', a mannequin, dressed in 1800 attire his hands tied behind his back. A reminder of days gone by. A few townspeople without imagination have on occasion tried to have George removed. "No go" say most folks. "It's a part of our colorful history." And indeed it is. George has been hangin' there for about 50 years. "It is very disturbing when George is taken down to have his clothes changed and given a bath" a local couple told us. People from as far away as Japan have voiced their opinion about 'George' to the local newspaper. He adds to the mystique of Placerville and the aura of the area" they wrote.

The stump from the old hangin' tree is still there too, in a crawl space under the building. Maybe it is not a good idea to go down there alone. Things still, do, go bump in the night on Main Street.

Have TWO drinks! The Hangtown Hangman still hangs and haunts his favorite place.

THE EMPIRE THEATRE
Gone, But Still There

It's a quiet walk down Main Street for you now. Traffic stopped when the stores closed for the night, and you feel very alone. Things seem somehow eerie. A strange swirling patch of cold wind passes you on an otherwise warm night in mid-July. The sound of ancient voices attract you to a building. You are taken by the vacant Empire Theatre, brick and beautiful as you pass by. Her doors were closed for the last time in April of 1997. Dark! The building seems enchanted, and once it was. The author, formerly a professional dancer, fantasizes how wonderful it would be if she were to open a performing arts studio there. Her credentials to do so are impeccable. As we go to press there is talk of using the building as a community theatre. But what about the ghosts..........

Originally the theatre was nothing more than a round tent where miners could entertain each other, and remember their days of culture. They often performed plays, some of the gruff men playing woman's parts, as women were few at the camps. In the late 1850's a wood structure was erected to replace the tent. It burned to the ground in the mid-1920's, and the now standing theatre built over it in the early 1930's. The old wood structure may have burned down, but it did not take the ghosts with it. Rumor has it they remained to stake their claim among the living theatre goers. They are stubborn too. Even after the theatre closed in April, they decided to stay.

Spirits are reported in the stage area of the building where it is believed a miner shot an opponent with a real pistol during one of the plays. No one seems to know if this was done intentionally or by mistake, but some folks say the poor bloke still stands on the stage, bullet in his chest. He does not seem to bother anyone, though if his shooter was around we suspect he might change his mind. The other acclaimed haunting is done by a spirit drunk who it is said to have suffered a heart attack in the boiler room. One prankster laid a bottle of brandy in the spot where the man died, only to find it empty the following morning. It is said some of the finest talent of the 1800's performed here, including Lotta Crabtree.

So if you pass the building and feel it's inhabitants, please say hello to the lonely ghosts. Its sad, and disheartening, to see the building empty of all but specters of the past. Such a lovely building. So much wonderful history.

PLACERVILLE COFFEE HOUSE (PEARSON'S SODA WORKS)
A Historic Building's Haunted History

Shadows glide effortlessly through the building. Spirits whisk by in the reflection, as employees clean store mirrors and windows. Labored breathing is heard permeating the thick rock walls of the empty old mine shaft inside the structure. Sometimes silverware is picked up by unseen hands and flung into the air as you enjoy your latte'. This certainly makes for interesting conversation. You think perhaps you should have ordered a double espresso instead. Well, sit back and enjoy. You have entered the Placerville Coffee House.

Located at 594 Main Street, we predict the old John McFarland Pearson Soda Works building will continue to cling fiercely to its rich memories. And why not? They are all here, you see. Everything lingers as if yesterday, because ghosts from the past mingle with the customers and employees of the present.

Built in 1859, (the upper portion in 1897 to bottle soda pop) the sturdy old brick and stone building must be saluted as it continues to serve the community, if in different capacities over so many years. Although some restoration was inevitable, the majority of the original is still the same, along with fixtures and keepsakes. The beautiful stained glass doors that greet you were brought here early on from a gambling hall in Montana. Among other things of interest to folks who lavish the past, and which add to the building's eerie allure, are hanging globes from the old San Francisco library, and marble bathroom fixtures from the ancient Tahoe Tavern. The building was used as a brewery, a soda works, and an ice cream parlor in the Gold Rush days, and more often than not, ice blocks, beer, soda, butter and other perishables, were stored in the 155 foot tunnel cut into the hill behind the place. The narrow mine tunnel at that time extended in a U-shape thru the mountain, ending near the Empire Theatre down the street. Much of it eventually caved in. It is said a second mine tunnel was started in an old house behind the Empire Theatre, and ran under Placerville, coming out somewhere in the vicinity of what is now Coloma Street. Deemed hazardous, it was eventually filled in.

Luckily for spirit trackers, the portion

inside the Placerville Coffee House is still intact. It's damp, it's drippy, and from sunset to sunrise it's also dark.

"Late one night in December of 1996, I was absentmindedly mulling around inside the mine shaft" said Mike Rideout, who along with his brother Pat opened the Placerville Coffee House in the historic building.
"My brother and I have several other businesses and were contemplating renting this place to start another. We just couldn't make up our minds. I think the landlord got sick of us, because he finally told us to take the keys and look things over for a couple of weeks until we made a decision. It was on one of the nights I was checking things out that I heard breathing coming from inside the walls of the mine." He stopped and gave me a big smile. "We had heard the stories about ghosts in the building from previous tenants, but not really being a believer, I thought my brother was playing a joke on me. I had come here by myself, but figured he must have followed, and somehow snuck in behind me. I went out and checked the doors but everything was still locked. I later learned he wasn't even in town. The only living person in the building was me."

That's not to say he was ALONE.

Stories about ghosts in this building have been told for many years. On this occasion we brought a psychic with us to see what her impressions would be. So well known for her exceptional work in spirit communication, we again inlisted the help of Rosemary Dean. Once inside the building she immediately gravitated toward the mine shaft. As she approached, a form appeared, slowly walking toward us from the depths and curves of the wet confines of the tunnel. The filmy form identified himself as

'Virgil'. "He was a miner, a young man of about 27 years, and he died in this cave" Rosie told us. "He was hit in the back of the head with a large rock. I am certain this happened during a minor cave-in. Unfortunately he was a victim." The entity yelled at us, and made a motion, pushing us back. "Do not go any further!" he said. "You don't belong here!"

The spirit then voiced his anger. "Didn't get my due" he told Rosie. " I have not been paid, not treated rightly!"

The ladies who are employed by the Placerville Coffee House told us of seeing ghosts in the mine area. "We often hear voices in the mine shaft" the employees continued. "They are either talking or fighting. Sometimes we hear the clattering of metal objects. When someone gets up the courage to go inside, it stops!"

Virgil is unaware he is dead. He spoke to us as if we lived in his day. He was quite surprised and dismayed we were wearing slacks. "Respectable women wear skirts" he told our psychic.

I asked Virgil if he knew he was dead. "No such thing" he responded. "I know where I am at. If I were dead I would not be here" he reasoned. He complained his head hurt. Because we could not see any signs of blood or bandaging, we asked him about his 'accident'. He stated he was not sure why his head hurt, but was certain he was not going anywhere until he got paid. "Nobody listens to me" he said, "And I want my money. I work hard for my money. Soon as I get paid, I will go get drunk and then get the wagon or if it's not there, I'll walk to there." He pointed in the direction of Newtown Road. " It's a long walk" he continued. "You know Jim! I live there with my Aunt and her child when I am not camped out. I like it at the farm. It's not my farm, but I grew up there."

He then changed the subject so we did not have a chance to ask him questions, connect the dots of his statements so to speak. He quickly began to complain about his lunch. "Where is my pail?" he asked someone we could not see. "Cheese is so expensive and I have bread and apples. I cannot find my pail and no one better have stolen my cheese!"

Rosie pointed at a spirit dog who rounded the corner from behind the register. He had been content to mingle with the assistants working behind the counter. Seeing Virgil he bounded toward us, happily reuniting with his friend. The dog, full of energy and jumping on the man excitedly, had obviously been waiting outside the mine shaft for his owner to return. "He's a troublemaker" Virgil told us. It was clear he was very fond of this brown, long ear, long tailed spotted dog. We left them playing at the entrance of the mine.

We continued our investigation by climbing the stairs to the upper portion of the building. Tables and easy chairs had been comfortably placed where light is good, so guests could read, eat, or enjoy their drinks in solitude or pleasant conversation. Not as rustic as downstairs, upstairs was homey, and gave us that feeling of belonging, like grandma's house. We sat at a table by a window looking out over the town, and enjoyed the quiet atmosphere. It was a rainy day, chilly outside, but the room was warm and cosy as Rosie tapped into the spirit of a man who liked to call himself the 'Mayor'. "He is a burly fellow with a mustache, and a straw hat for which he is noted. He likes to stay around and have fun with people" Rosie said. Quite an organizer, he held meetings here. This chubby man died of a heart attack, and not only is here at the building, but comes and goes as he feels like it. Several of his cronies are here as well, as they banter and tell tales of the times.

"A waste of time" an older woman in the building told us about the men. Skinny, dressed in the style of the 1800, she seemed distant, perhaps a bit slow. She hissed at us, showing her displeasure. "This is my place, you don't belong here!" She told us her name was Alice, she then walked past us, slipped through the door to the women's restroom, telling us it was her intent to clean it.

The miner in the cave enjoys his friends and faithful dog.

Two security guards stopped at the Placerville Coffee House on their way home from work one day, and were startled to see silverware being picked-up by unseen hands, and flung across the room. One man employed at the Coffee House told the author he went upstairs to the men's room, and as he approached, the door slammed in his face. "This has happened to other people as well" he told us. "And it happens all the time. We don't know why." Our experts feel it is unlikely there is an 'earthly' explanation, as the door was stuck the day we were there. If that is how it still is, the door will probably need to be shaved in order to swing smoothly. "Once you get in, the room seems to want to 'push' you out as well" the man said.

We enjoyed the Placerville Coffee House. It does have ghosts, and it does have charm, and it now has our new friends, Mike and Pat, who, undaunted, intend to stay. The already thriving business has many, (if you'll excuse the pun,) perks. There are wonderful musical groups, guitars, and other important talents there to entertain. Week-ends are happening, with live music and "storytellers". The Placerville Coffee House sells wonderful goodies, great coffees, cappaccino, smoothies, mochas, offers full espresso and juice bars, bagels, rolls, danish, and fresh soups daily. Banquet and meeting rooms are also available. It's the perfect place to take your shoes off and commune with friends, do your homework, relax after a busy day and chatter with the employees. And maybe, if you believe, a spirit or two.. But then, you really should see for yourself!

As we left the building we waved to Virgil, still sitting where we left him, his arm around his dog.

"Get some skirts on!" he told us.

NOTE: The Placerville Coffee House is
located At:
        594 Main Street
        Placerville, CA. 95667
        (530) 295-1481

CHAMBER OF COMMERCE BUILDING
Update on a Very Haunted Place

If you go to the Chamber of Commerce
building at 542 Main Street in Placerville
and ask for directions to some of the most
interesting places to see in this historic
town, the employees may very well put their
arms around you and show you their own work
place. Without much begging, they might take
you up the stairs to where the ghost most
likes to "hang" out. And then they will tell
you their stories.

Researched extensively for Gold Rush
Ghosts #1 which hit the book stores in 1990,
the accountings were originally brought to
our attention by Debi Cayer, former
Assistant Vice President and Branch Manager
of Central Pacific Mortgage, who worked in
the building from 1979 to July of 1981. "The
ghost in the building was felt by people
working with me, loan officers, and other
employees. People have certainly
experienced the ghost and believe the
building is haunted."

While having our conversation with Cayer,
another person in the building wanted to
share his experience with us. "I want to
add that one evening while I was alone
upstairs, I heard strange banging sounds, as
if someone was bumping and crashing into the
furniture. I called out but no one answered.
Then I remembered I was alone in the place.

I couldn't wait to get out of there!"

Often these type of occurrences can be explained logically. In the case of the Chamber building, this is just not so.

Investigations produce nothing. There are no rats in the walls making noise. Bats are not flying thru the building. Buzzing sounds are not coming from swarms of bees in a colony. The old Chamber building hides many secrets, phantoms if you will, swaggering, disobedient spirits. Over the past 15 years, employees are always grateful when Placerville City Police respond quickly to their calls. They then report seeing a slightly transparent man with whiskers and top hat lingering in the balcony. They have a right to be "spooked." They have tapped into the "other" world, one we know very little about. We were amazed to find the building had been built over a large tree used for hangings during the Gold Rush days. Marian Watry, former General Manager of the El Dorado Chamber, and who worked in the building for many years, told us the ghost was mostly seen around the mezzanine, which was the exact height of the limb from which many men were hanged... In 1981-1982 the mezzanine was covered over by a dropped ceiling to allow for lighting accommodations. When we spoke to her in 1987 she explained the ghost put up quite a fuss. The combined consensus of the employees is the ghost is that of the official "Hangman" from the Gold Rush days. Obviously the "Hangman" is not one who likes things to change. The workman dealt with plumbing problems in the building, tools disappearing only to be found on another floor, and serious disturbances that could have cost the contractor his time and money. Since our first book was released, the ghost has not let up his pace. We thought a visit with our psychic Rosemary Dean would be in order, especially since she had already pegged him at the Hangman's Bar, her own Fairchild building, and in this structure as well. The annoying specter did not disappoint us. What we encountered was more than we expected, and a foreboding reminder of a pale shadowy apparition, the dead man's life, and some of his thoughts.

It was a rainy, dismal day. We approached the building with Rosie, Pat Kenyon, an Intuitive Consultant, Healer and Energy Therapist, and our photographer. Approaching the stairs, the building seemed suddenly cold, especially in the corners. "He's here" Rosie told us. "I believe he divides his time between the three places. He walks the streets, unaware of anything around him. He has a job to do and he does it well. He is very grim."

"Not that he never smiles" she was quick to add. "He could smile. Usually in the company of men, his buddies. He was definitely a man's man, related better to that gender, you know the type. He feels the weight of his actions, very guilty about taking lives."

"And he feels badly for his misplaced judgements as well" she continued, lost in the world of the Hangman. "To justify what he did he had to think of the victims as nothing more than scum. In his heart he realized all people were people, and all his victims had lives. Some lost them rightfully, some not. I believe his job and his attitude toward it eventually caused him to have a heart attack."

Kathleen Dodge, the pretty brunette Film Commissioner for the El Dorado County Film Commission, and who's office is upstairs directly in the path of the once swinging rope, told us sometimes she feels invisible eyes looking at her when she is alone in her office. "I refuse to be intimidated" she said. "But there is definitely someone here, and they want you to know it."

"I believe the 'Hangman' feels a certain rapport with Kathleen Dodge" Rosie told us. "He likes her 'no nonsense and 'take charge' personality. She cannot be pushed around, and he feels it is alright to be in her presence without disturbing her." Rosie assured the employees in the building that he is not dangerous, or evil, though most have gotten used to his presence. " He's just upset" she told them." At himself, at the building, and at things in general. His occupation was a grim one, and he did it well, for better or worse. She suggested a tape recorder be left on in the building over night. "He just might want to communicate with you" she said.

For the employees of the Chamber who work downstairs, things are either bizarre or exciting, depending how you look at it. Imagine never knowing what you are going to walk into when you come to work in the morning. "Papers move about and sometimes we cannot find them after they have been filed or put away" Shirly Richards, Manager of Business Services for the Chamber told us. "We are always feeling someone is behind us, but when we look we are alone. Strange noises are heard all the time, in empty rooms and above us. Things fall off desks and crash to the floor. We are forever tripping over items on the floor that were not there before. You don't take anything for granted around here. Things are forever being mysteriously moved. Every day is a new adventure."

"One Saturday I was working alone in the building when I was lucky enough to catch a glimpse of him out of the corner of my eye"

Richards told us. " All of us are aware of the ghosts in this building."

Pat Kenyon was able to communicate with several entities that the Chamber was previously unaware of. Both are from a later time than the 'Hangman', and neither seem to associate with him or care about his presence. "One's name is Tom" she told us. "I believe his last name began with a"B". His father had a lot to do with the construction or upkeep of the building. He grew up around this building, playing in and out of the rooms and stairs." She tuned in to the spirit. "He says he lived here about 40 years ago. He died in an accident. He loves the place, and just stays around because he was happy here. The other is a woman from the 1800s, and her name is Agnes.

It would be an interesting study to anyone who wanted to trace the stories of these people. Especially "Tom." Who was he, why does he love the building so, and why does he refuse to go on to what is supposed to be a better dimension? Surprises, surprises, surprise. Each time we enter the Chamber of Commerce building it is like opening Pandora's Box.

Placerville C of C Building.   Look up and see the Hangman!

NOTE: Further information on the Chamber of Commerce Building in Placerville is available in <u>Gold Rush Ghosts #1.</u>
The Chamber of Commerce building is located at: 542 Main Street
Placerville, CA. 95667
(530) 621-5885

THE FAIRCHILD BUILDING
The Uppermost in Upstairs Ghosts

In a dim lit hall, being warmed by a long gone potbelly stove, the remnants of an old timer sits on a wooden barrel, his face flushed from heat. He puts his hands out to feel the intensity, then rubs them together. He is comfortable here, and gives no indication he wants to move on. The problems he had in the physical life still 'kick in' from time to time, his headaches, sinus infections, and at one point he sniffles to end the annoyance. Mostly he is glad to be out of the cold. That damn, miserable cold! He has told our psychic Rosemary Dean that his name is Joe, and that he has been here a long time. He is a 'salt of the earth' type of fellow, and does not mind having his space invaded by the folks that now use the building. In fact, he loves the company and even has his favorites among the owner and his renters. He says he also enjoys another building on the same block, and warms his frozen hands in front of that long gone potbelly stove as well. But he does love the upstairs unit of the stately Fairchild Building. And although there are two businesses that occupy the downstairs, the upstairs at 429 Main Street is where this ghost seem to be most content. It is upstairs, here, he plays his little tricks and games. And, if you think his antics are not enough, there are many other spirit folks as well. But don't dally now. Lets take the trek.

Not to be confused, there are two Fairchild buildings on Main Street in Placerville. The one we are visiting is just a short walk from the Hangman's Tree. The gray building, originally built around 1854, served the community in many capacities over the years. It is believed to have been a mortuary, hospital, a row of doctors offices, and a cat house in the 1800s, and now houses several businesses and offices including world famous Rosemary Dean's.

We enter through the wooden door, and climb the 24 steps to the second landing. To the right we see our Psychic Rosie's office, pink and cheery. We wonder how many lives she has helped by giving them back their loved ones, or securing their future. Just today a woman called with a thank you. Told by Rosie she was going to have a massive heart attack and should move closer to a town with a hospital from her estate in the woods of Georgetown, she called to say she was glad she took Rosie's advise. Her heart attack came two weeks ago and if she had not gotten immediate medical attention she would have died.

There are sixteen other rooms in the upstairs of the Fairchild building, including two bathrooms. The rooms are rented by several interesting people, including a massage therapist and Astrological Counselor, and although some of the rooms are used for storage, the spirits don't seem to discriminate. They visit them all.

I remember a first visit to Rosie's office. She was with a client, so I sat down in a chair in front of the office just across the hall from her's. The room now occupies a Hair Stylists, but at the time it was vacant.

Soon I smelled the distinct odor of smoke coming from inside the room. I tried the door but it was locked. Dark smoke escaped, billowing out from under the door.

Alarmed, I ran to Rosie's office, and not waiting to knock, interrupted her session. "Rosie, there is a fire in the room across from yours!"

She smiled at me "No, I have seen it too, but there is no fire" she said.

"Well, smell the smoke" I besieged her. "Call the fire department!"

"I know" she said, "But nothing is wrong."

Knowing Rosie over the years, I have learned to trust her judgement, although it was an uneasy fifteen minutes for me waiting for her to finish with her client.

When she did, she went to see the owner of the building, who's office is next door to her's, and asked if we could be let in to the room. Jim Newmeyer, in his gracious way, agreed and grabbing the key, put it into the lock. There was certainly a smell of smoke, and an swaggering haze, but no signs of a recent fire. "Yes", he told us, "I can smell the smoke. But there is no fire. Nothing is hot or even warm." I looked at him curiously. "I was told that many years ago there was a fire in this room" he told me. Rosie looked at him knowingly. "The smell must still be from that time." Well, maybe so, but it does not account for the smoke that is seen by many people, at all times of the day or night. It was an interesting day, and one I will never forget.

I soon learned Rosie's evening classes can also be spooky. In Rosie's room it is carte blanche for ghosts, those who'live'in the building, and those who come to visit. It is like visiting a different world, which in reality it is. They come through the door open or shut. There are people, animals and things...........A wonderful experience.

The hangman from down the street at the Hangman's Tree shows his dispirited self to the occupants as well. It is when Rosie is alone in her office late at night he seems to want the most attention. He is often seen in the upstairs hallway, dressed as we have seem him in other buildings, and with the same stern look on his face. What he does in his spare time is of no consequence to us though we doubt if he is still hangin' folks. He seems content to walk the buildings and the streets and watch, always watch, what is taking place. Perhaps, after all, he is looking for his next victim.

"There is the child on the step" Rosie was to tell us. "It is the third step, and we often trip over him. Sometimes he is crying and I wonder what he is doing there, but if I pry, he turns and walks away."

The ghosts of the Fairchild building are strong and worthy of investigation to anyone going up the stairs for an appointment or to visit the renters. Have fun, experience, and come out enlightened. But don't get in the way of the invisible potbelly stove. Joe is trying to keep warm!

NOTE: The Fairchild Building is located at:
      429 Main Street
      Placerville, CA. 95667
      Rosemary Dean's Office
      (530) 626-5138

5

DIAMOND SPRINGS
Devilish Diggins' With A Past

This quaint community located two and one half miles south of Placerville, and two miles northeast of El Dorado, still boasts a few buildings that date back to the Gold Rush era. Two worth mentioning are the I.O.O.F. Hall, built in 1852, and the old Wells Fargo Express office. First called Crystal Springs, the area was the original site of Sutter's split shakes mill, and the town swelled and deflated in accordance with the prosperity of the business. Crystal Springs was officially considered a good bet for placer claims by 1849, as many emigrants found themselves camping on this route, a major trail from the Sierra Nevada. As if on cue, fires erupted in the Gold Rush Days, often leveling whole blocks of city buildings, in Placerville, Georgetown, Kelsey, Grizzley Flat, Newtown, and many others. In 1856 Diamond Springs suffered a major blow as hastily build dwellings and quality structures were leveled to the ground. No matter now. As you will see, many prospectors, ranch hands and business owners survived the fires and the destructive nature of the times. Some are still here to tell us about them.

THE DIAMOND SPRINGS HOTEL
Happy, Homespun, and Haunted

The Diamond Springs Hotel, which sits near the sight of an old Miwok Indian Crematorium, is considered one of the finest down home country places to eat in all the Gold Rush Country. It's popularity is credited to the fine food served by new owners Dan & Carole Dummett. The business is often hurried in a 'laid back' sort of way, with customers and friends, all enjoying their conversations as they wait for their meals. The atmosphere is friendly and warm as you are greeted by 'Diamond' Dan and Carole and the old timers of the town who will treat you as if you are family. And if you listen very carefully, you just might overhear them talking about the "strange things" that happen inside the building. And if you ask, they might even tell you about the ghosts that have become a part of the woodwork.

Originally built in 1916 by Antone Meyer, the business was cared for by his son Carl until 1932 when it was sold to John Zannoni. The building was used, through a series of owners, as a hotel upstairs, and at different times a bar, store, or restaurant on the bottom level. And although the building itself brings in many ghosts, because of it's natural vortex (try standing with eyes closed in the middle of the room), most of the ghostly apparitions are there since the time before the hotel was built.

"We do not know what causes a vortex" Psychic Pat Kenyon was to explain to us. "We do know that it is an opening in the earth's surface where spirit can access.
It can be explained as pores in the body.
It is a place where energy can be fed, a

natural doorway for entities to come in and out, a change or higher place of energy, a comfortable place for spirits, a neutral area." She stopped for a moment, composing her thoughts as she tried to further explain the phenomena known as vortex. "It may seem unnatural to some people" she told us, "But there are vortexes all over the world. Some are stronger than others. The one at the site of the Diamond Springs Hotel is very solid, firm, powerful, creating an atmosphere of ease for many entities to enter and exit."

In 1847 the town now known as Diamond Springs was originally called Crystal Springs, the name attributed to the beautiful spring water that fed the area. According to Dennis Witcher, Curator of the El Dorado County Historic Museum in Placerville, "The area which now houses the Diamond Springs Hotel was the site of Sutter's original split shakes mill." It was also a camp for miners and weary travelers, some slept on the ground, others in homemade tents. These people, long deceased to this world anyway, with the comfortablity of the vortex, can return to this place without stress, floating into our world and back to their own with record ease. And we know that many do, and bring their friends as well.

But back to the current, while dealing with the past, waitresses at the Diamond Springs Hotel tell us of the uncanny occurrences that make their days more exasperating than the average servers jobs. The kind that arouse the senses, make the adrenaline flow a bit faster than usual, and keep you looking over your shoulder as you prepare to open the business in the morning.

"I often hesitate to go into the corner by the restrooms when I first get here in the morning" Nancy Miller was to tell the author. "I will be alone in the building and things just go haywire. First of all I will hear noises inside the restrooms. I race into the men's room and fill the dispensers, do whatever is needed, and get the heck out. Sometimes there is a faint damp odor that I cannot explain. All the while I will have that unescapable feeling that someone is watching me." She smiled at us with that great sense of humor she possesses. "For all this trouble, I hope he's at least Good lookin'" she whispered. At other times things do not go as planned at the servers station in the same section, which is about the middle of the building. "You put a jelly or syrup down, turn around, and poof it has disappeared!" Again, it is believed, because the natural vortex is in the the back corner by the restrooms, this area is especially conducive to spirit activity. Try and explain this to the employees as reason for the unearthly activity to be considered commonplace. Often folks have been known to see a filmy figure of a man sitting in the back booth with his big black lab at his side. Upon wondering why a dog would be in a restaurant, they look up to find an empty table.

"He was a rather crotchety kind of guy, and is here from the Gold Rush days" Pat Kenyon was to tell us. "He is comfortable sitting in the booth and watching people. It is near the spot he pitched his tent in 1843. He had cancer of the stomach, knew he was dying, and worried about his two children, both girls, left with relatives in Oregon." She raised her hand as if to hold his. "The man's name is Matthew, and he calls his dog Butch. They enjoy watching people eat because he was denied that

82

pleasure at the end of his life. He likes the girls at the restaurant and is amazed by the job they do. He is always happy to see them coming in the morning, and regrets their leaving at night."

The upstairs rooms at the Diamond Springs Hotel is now used for storage and an office for Diamond D. It beckons and groans, bangs and clashes whenever it feels so disposed. Early in the days of the hotel, and thru several restorations, the building endured many changes. We have learned through our research that most spirits insist on steadfastness, being more comfortable with the familiar. "I think they are putting up a fuss" Kenyon stated, "Even though I have told them that the new owners are not responsible for those changes." She assured us, and the spirits of this fact. The owners often wonder who, or what, is making all the commotion.

Diamond Hotel- Diamond Dan and his non-paying guests. They take up booths but don't order from the menu.

"I see a man sitting on a bed" Kenyon said, "And a woman crying. They are fighting, arguing. The kids are upstairs and in the kitchen area. They can cause quite a fuss. There is one now, downstairs, at the corner booth, waving at the guests in the banquette room." A waitress was to tell us she went to open the door to the outside patio and felt the door 'Flying out of my hands' as if someone unseen had pulled it from the other side. "That would be the eldest child, about fourteen years old. They are very prankish" Said Kenyon. They also love to harass the kitchen help, leaving water on, dropping dishes, or fooling with the electricity. The activity seems to increase as the day goes on. "You can expect the plumbing to give you stress in the near future" Kenyon stated. "They seem to be fooling with that now."

Jeri Moser, also a waitperson at the Diamond Springs Hotel shared her story with Gold Rush Ghosts. "This will clear up some of what happened upstairs to my husband, children and me" she said. "For two and a half years we rented the apartment upstairs from the restaurant. One of the cardinal rules, written in the rental contract was that the children were not to run in the apartment. Well, one day Carole and I were downstairs and we heard running upstairs. I went to yell at the kids but Carole said she was sure the noise did not come from the apartment. It was coming from the storage area next to it. When she went to investigate, it was still locked. There was no way my children could have gotten in there considering it was locked from the outside and all. And, it was not just us that heard the running, but all the employees as well." She stopped to compose her thoughts. "Another time I was in the

84

shower. I felt a presence get into the tub with me, and put his fingers in my long brown hair. I thought it was my husband, but when I turned around to give him a smile, there was no one there. That was really spooky."

"Another night my husband and I heard crying coming from the room Diamond Dan used as his office. We also heard what we thought to be a cat knocking things off a metal shelf. We brought it to Dan's attention in the morning, but when he went to check, nothing was amiss.

"We moved out a few months ago, and because I am often the last to leave in the evening after my shift, I looked up at the upstairs windows as I got into my car. The light was on in Dan's old office. It was off in the morning when the next shift came in" she told us, "Because I inquired about it. Several days later a couple came in and asked me who was living upstairs now? They had seen the light in the old office on several nights in a row." There is no one living upstairs at the Hotel now, and certainly not in the old abandoned office. At least no one living.

Sherry Alicea, another server at the Diamond Springs Hotel was to share her story with us. " There was an evening as I was closing up for the night that was very strange. All the customers were out of the restaurant, and the few lingering were on the deck. I had just come in through the kitchen area and was startled as I entered the dining room. It was misty, the whole room was covered in fog. It was the most remarkable thing I have ever seen." She pointed in the direction of the vortex. "I do stumble a lot over there" she told us. "Seems like something is always in my way."
What would seem natural, but

unfortunately absent, is any sighting of entities seemingly associated with the crematorium down the road. It is those legendary rowdy miners of the era, and their friends, that continue to thrive among the living and make themselves at home in the Diamond Springs Hotel. Diamond Dan and Carole see no reason, as yet, to have them removed.

For all the ghosts that run through the Diamond Springs Hotel, it remains one of the coziest places in El Dorado County.

"We just take what happens in stride" Carole said. "Everyone is welcome here" she told us. "Paying customers and the others as well."

NOTE: The Diamond Hotel is located at: 545
Pleasant Valley Road
Diamond Springs, CA. 95619

6.

GHOSTS UP THE HILL
Georgetown and Garden Valley

Mining soon progressed up the hill. With so many men with their feet in the rivers and streams, the more industrious took to the mountains. They migrated in groves out of the muck and into the snakes, poison oak and wild animals. When this form of mining brought color, many dug in and stayed. International developers from around the world sent representatives to survey the country. They asked questions and made charts concerning the most likely places to find gold. Upon reporting their findings, large convoys of people from around the globe privy to this information descended upon the virtually untouched beauty that was the wild country. Lode mines shot up as fast as you could tie your shoes. Many also ceased operation almost as soon as they started. The American Heritage Dictionary of the English Language, New Dell Edition, First Printing July 1980, defines 'lode' as a vein of mineral ore deposited between layers of rock. Often a 'vein' would be found, and mines would appear within a quarter mile from the first mine, along the same vein, stretching for miles. Many mines prospered, bringing needed dollars to the small communities that popped up with familiar urgency. Others were as quickly

87

abandoned, left to rot as gold seekers moved to richer ground.

The nip of fall was in the air when two men, George and Stephen Pierce, purchased a plot of land high above Coloma in 1849. Their plan was different. They put on their heavy jackets and dug into the soil, not this time to secure gold, but to plant seeds. Spring and Summer came, and their garden prospered. Their plan had worked, they would sell needed vegetables to neighboring camps. Years later they were to sell their land to the McConnell brothers, who changed the place into a trading post, where they continued to sell their goods. The brothers then purchased another stretch of land close to the first with their money. The land was rich and that plot also prospered, yielding much more than they could ever imagine. In 1852 a 4th of July celebration was held, and the McConnell brothers, owners of the trading post, donated all the vegetables for the festivities. It was at this occasion that a vote was taken. This area rich in soil, should be called Garden Valley. A post office was established, and Garden Valley became a town.

A beautiful town, and lucky to still out of the way of progress, it has changed very little over the years. It is small in numbers, and still boasts many lush gardens. The hills are peppered with pines and oak and brush. Neighbors still wave to each other as they pass, as no one is a stranger. Sometimes the men folk sit around and talk about the good old days. Sometimes they talk about the ghosts.

REMNANTS OF THE ROSECRANS(Z) MINE
See It While You Can

Greenwood is the only major road that runs through Garden Valley. Two small lanes that weave their way to the next little town, and then to Hyw. 193. For ghost purposes, Greenwood Road can most easily be reached by coming up Marshall Road (or the old Prospector Road) from Coloma/Lotus. It is the first major left turn at the top of the hill. The new fire station is on the corner.

As you travel about 100 yards down this paved yet narrow country byway, you notice the many old homes and out-buildings which still dot the hills in this part of the Gold Rush country. Around one such major curve, you slow, because you think you see it through in the fog. Almost invisible behind the trees in the woods, to the left of the road you see a crumbling imposing building. Yes, it is a mine. And as you view the mine you are certain you see activity surrounding it. But you don't. You have entered the realm of the Rosecrans(z) Mine. Let your mind wander.

Lost through time we do not know why it was named the Rosecrans(z). It is made in the old tradition of cement and wood, and was originally three stories high. Time, as with all things have taken their toll on the Rosecrans. You are glad you chose to see it now, because each year it crumbles further, courtesy of the rains and wind that come in fall and winter. If you could get up closer you would know the rotted base will soon give way. The remaining Rosecrans will then cease to stand, because like people and all other things abandoned and forgotten, it cannot survive without proper care and maintenance. That day will be a tragedy for history, and for the Rosecrans.

In its day this mine was not a hearty producer of gold, especially in comparison to other mines in the area. Its major accomplishment was in 1888 when it hit its peak by producing $21,000 in gold ore, yielded #10 per ton. Originally worked to an inclined depth of 200 feet, and then closed down. It reopened for three years, from 1936 to 1939, and then ceased operation for good. Records show that no further substantial find was pulled from the earth in the vicinity surrounding the Rosecrans Mine.

What sets this mine apart from the others, is as far back as the community can remember, strange perverse sounds and flickering lights have been observed from the abandoned edifice. On summer evenings, in the stillness, banging can be heard, as if someone is still working the mine. Busy laughter fills the air. Ah, an authoritative voice and the laughter stops. Hammers pound invisible nails. We enter to investigate. No one is there. Nothing has been moved or altered. No old timbers have fallen. There are no footprints in the dirt. A baffled community looks for answers to this eerie yet unexplainable phenomena. Many of the residents of the area continue to be frightened by the unknown.

A long dirt path exists through the woods adjacent to the Rosecrans. A few years ago two teenage brothers, along with their parents, moved into the house at the end of the driveway. Wishing to investigate their new surroundings, they took their dog, a well-bred German Shepherd down the long path and through to the brush. The dog strutted ahead of his master, chasing birds and jutting in and out of the underbrush. Occasionally he would chase a squirrel through the woods, and then reappear. It was one of those lazy beautiful days that all kids who grow up in the country experience.

And then they heard it!

The dog, repositioning himself before the children, abruptly stopped. He refused to continue down the path. His fur raised on his back, and he circled his masters, pushing them back. Should he attack? If so, what?......

"We heard the sound of earth moving" the boys told us. "It was like something collapsing. Then we heard clanging and one loud bang," the older brother said, excitedly. "I held my dog so he wouldn't go running off. We heard the sounds of someone working at that old abandoned mine," he said. "There was hammering and voices. Then it all faded away, slowly getting softer until we couldn't hear it anymore." The younger brother fiddled with the lining of his jacket as he remembered what happened. "The dog seemed confused as to what was going on. We could see nothing strange, and yet there were these sounds. Something was happening, and yet it wasn't" he said.

"In that split second, the dog did something he had never done before, and hasn't done since" the boys told us. "He put his tail between his legs and took off for home. We were not far behind him!"

"I have heard it too" stated a pretty 19 year old honor student from Garden Valley. "I also saw the light."

For all intent, the mine displays a mysterious light which shows itself at all times of the evening, in any time of year and in all weather, but most predominantly in the fall. It can be elusive, but most always hovers to the left side of the mine head and crasher section of the old

91

building. When not seen plainly it is encased in an ectoplasmic fog.

The teenager had one more story of the light, and was anxious to tell about her experience. "At a little past one a.m.," she began, "My friend Bob King and I were on our way home from a party at the house at the end of the dirt road. Some other friends were to have returned and picked us up, but they forgot us. I had a curfew so we had to walk. As we approached the mine we were startled by a loud crash inside the building. I grabbed Bob. We stood in the shadows for a long time, quiet, just watching to see what it was. My heart was pounding as it was pretty dark there in the woods. Just as we were getting ready to resume our walk, I thought I saw someone move in front of the window and there was an eerie light came on from inside the mine building." She hesitated a moment, so mature for her years, and wanting to give a good and complete description. "The light was a misty white and it seemed to hover and glow. It was an oblong shape, and as I said, hovered. From side to side. Slowly!" She waited patiently for me to adjust the tape recorder. "Bob started throwing rocks at the mine, because we thought, well, we were hoping anyway, that someone was there playing a trick on us. If there was someone there, they surely would have been hurt by those rocks, or throwing some back, or begging us to stop. No one answered. This is a remote area and there was obviously no one around. Bob held on to my hand and we ran the remaining half mile to my home. Later I learned that many people have seen the mysterious light at the Rosecrans Mine."

As if the ghostly mine, with all its inhabitants were not enough, the Rosecrans keeps another secret as well. The Rosecrans is also frequented by a phantom voice in the night, a helpless soul whose's screams plead for mercy from one of the many holes which are death traps to the unsuspecting victim who does not know their whereabout. Those in the know do not venture beyond the crude barb wire fence that has been erected haphazardly around the danger areas. In the community's laid back way, no warning signs are posted, or if they have been, are not visible. The mine is now on private property, reason in itself to not venture. It is known that years ago open stopes were used all along the old shaft, both to the north and south of it, and the holes are now filled in with water and debris yielded by the forest. It is here, at one of these holes, this poor, helpless soul seems to repeat his own horrible death. He is heard over and over again, year after year. What quirk of fate could decree such terrible punishment, and when and who can put his anguish to rest? It is not to strange of a tale that no mention in the archives or old newspapers could be found concerning a death from drowning at the Rosecrans. Many people disappeared at the time of the Gold Rush, some mysteriously. Few records were kept. We wonder which one, and who, is our suffering soul?

"It's eerie and strange being around there" said Bob King, 21 years old at the time of our interview. He had another encounter with the unimaginable while walking near the mine. A rock hound, he was looking at the ground when he heard the voice of someone close by.

"I heard a frantic 'help', a mumbled voice as if drowning, and then coming up for air." King shuttered as he told the story. "I ran to the only spot close that I knew was a hole in the ground. The voice had been coming from this direction." He quietly remembered the unthinkable. "There could have been no one drowning in that hole. At least not the day I was there. The murky water in the hole had not been disturbed as was evident in the scum that was still unmoved on the top.

"Again I heard the cries of a man drowning...going up and down again, into that hole...." he remembered well. "It happened again louder, and it sounded like a man fighting for air. I called out "Where are you?" Not really wanting a reply, because deep down I knew what I had heard was not normal, the sound of someone actually in trouble, right now, today. It sounded too distant, too strange." He looked up thoughtfully. "I needn't have worried. There was no reply. In fact, as I remember I got an uneasy feeling in my stomach because the forest had become completely silent, not even a cricket, or bird was making a sound. I started to leave, but was increasingly aware of the leaves rustling under my feet because of the strange silence. I stood still for what seemed a long time, but was probably just a minute or two. Slowly the sounds of birds, bugs, leaves, normal forest sounds came back. I was happy when the activity returned. I swear to you, not so much as a leaf fell to the ground when the voice was there. I was never so glad as when I reached the road, the sun hit my face, and I heard the sound of cars coming in my direction. Civilization!" He thought for a moment, then spoke softly. "I will go back one day" he told the author. "I would go back with you, the sheriff, or the photographer you have with you. Maybe with friends. But I won't go alone!"

It is certain this unimportant mine, of

little other consequence, will be remembered in ways that surrendered riches in gold as one still holding the secrets of those personalities that refuse to die as even the last timber falls to the earth and the last metal roofing plank is stolen by some industrious rancher eager to build his own new barn at the expense of history. The Rosecrans is haunted. Not by what, but whom, and why, we do not know.

Traveling five miles uphill from Garden Valley, you will find the neighboring town of Georgetown. Georgetown is still somewhat untouched in spirit (excuse the pun) as an 1800's town. Of cause there are those bullheads who try to clean'er up, and bring a conversion to modern day life. Unfortunately, as in most cases, this is done for the sake of making a buck, and at the expense of a beautiful past. From those we have spoken to, Georgetown won't go down easy for the count. Nothing runs by the book in Georgetown, and if you think I'm lying, ask any sheriff who patrols the country. We were there the day an official tried to stop folks from parking their cars in the middle of the road when they couldn't find a conventional parking place. We all know change is inevitable, but hats off to the rednecks and old-timers who fight for their way of life. They venomously resist change, and we applaud their courage as individuals. God love them!

Any Georgetownite will tell you their town is believed to be the source of the ever-familiar rumor giving California the reputation of having streets paved in gold. The town was originally called Growlersburg as the nuggets mined were often ten ounces or more. Miners called them growlers, insisting they made a growling noise when swirled in the pans. Nuggets were found everywhere, under the roots of trees, rocks after storms, and in all the rivers, streams and gulches. There are stories of settler women buying store bought roses, digging a hole and finding a nugget large enough to buy a new homestead, and employ a full time gardener.

Georgetown sprang up around 1849 when ten to twenty-five thousand miners heard that 2,000 or more nuggets were reportedly found within its hills. Most of the men made their way from the American River. Some came from back east, afraid to take the original trek to Coloma, but with more courage now. Hadn't Uncle George sent a letter saying how well he was doing 'out west?'

As common in all the mining settlements in the Mother Lode, Georgetown was also ravaged with fires. Over and over again. In 1852 the town laid out one-hundred-foot wide streets to serve as fire breaks. Unfortunately their efforts were of little help as they watched the business district destroyed soon after. In 1897 a cache of dynamite exploded, spewing debris as far away as two miles. True to the determined nature of the residents of Georgetown today, they began the rebuilding as fast as the fire cooled. There are those that still pick up good size chunks of gold around Georgetown. And since the beginning, there has always been a Georgetown Hotel.

THE GEORGETOWN HOTEL
Pranks, Peanuts, and Paybacks

Your walk into yesterday begins as you enter the building. You are met with the aura of the 1800's, as you might have imagined it, old tables, stools at the bar, and until recently peanuts on the floor. It was not too long ago that <u>Gold</u> <u>Rush</u> <u>Ghosts</u> encountered a man at the bar drinking beer from a mason jar, his trusty friend, Max the dog, besides him. High atop the stool, ole' Max had his own brew. No one seemed to notice anything uncommon. Most folks just ate their peanuts and flicked the shells to the floor. Soon a man came through the door on the back of his horse. He handed the bartender his jar, and it was filled to the top. He gave a salute and exited the building the same way he came, and proceeded to ride off as they say, 'into the sunset'. In this case, that consisted of riding his saddled mount down the middle of the two lane road. Ah the country!

But that was in the really good old days. With health laws being enforced now, things have changed a bit. Damn regulations. Still, the atmosphere is the same, and you wonder as you look at the old artifacts hanging on the walls, how much history the building has seen, and remembered. The Georgetown Hotel has been around since Georgetown itself. It was built, and rebuilt, after every devastating fire that swept through town. This more than century old hotel is a treat, with a downstairs bar, upstairs rooms for rent, and over the years on occasion, a restaurant. The upstairs rooms even had iron beds and muslin curtains the last time we looked. Bath and showers were down the hall, and we knew it was more a place to absorb atmosphere than to enjoy luxuries. Such are the ways of Georgetown.

Years ago, folks at the Georgetown Hotel liked to boast it was the only hotel in the United states to have a room 13. A recent bartender told this author the Georgetown Hotel no longer advertises this. But,

fearless friends, several other hotels from
our travels do. The folks at the
Georgetown Hotel may or may not be
superstitious, but the room formerly known
as room 13 is thought to have a ghost
inside. And, the elusive spirit roams the
rest of the place when he is bored. He
takes great pride in controlling the
kitchen, especially when it is cluttered. It
is then he can play his pranks. And if you
get on his bad side, he has been known to
drop a drink on you, fling something off the
shelf, or find other ingenious yet
uncomfortable ways to let you know he is
there. It is deeply suspected the
transparent entity is the remains of a
previous owner who died in one of the major
holocausts to beset early Georgetown. It is
believed he probably lost his life in the
1897 fire which whipped through town like a
mugger on the run, destroying everything in
its path.

Cooks at the hotel told us during our
investigation for <u>Gold Rush Ghosts #1</u> in
1990, of seeing him numerous times,
sometimes directly in front of them and
sometimes out of the corner of their eyes.
They say he stands in the kitchen or by the
heater in the bar. "He usually has his hands
on his hips as if analyzing the place," they
told the author. "He is an older man,
perhaps fifty years of age, tall and with
salt and pepper colored hair. He has a pipe
in his mouth. Sometimes when I go to the
kitchen in the morning," one of the chefs
told us, "things will be rearranged. I will
have to go looking for pots and pans,
spatulas and such. Being the last one to
leave the night before, and having locked up
myself, I know no one else could have done
it. Then I look up, and he is there,
staring at me. I blink my eyes, and he is

gone. My heart does a double take. It is frightening, and a big annoyance."

According to Bobbie Thompson, former co-owner of the hotel, in an article written by this author for the <u>Georgetown</u> <u>Gazette</u> in 1983, "The television set downstairs will go on by itself in the middle of the night, and lights will go on and off without reason." He certainly enjoys playing games.

"Apparently the old gentleman had a small dog," said Thompson, "because he has also been seen." When redecorating the building, after pulling off layers of wallpaper, Thompson came across a letter written in the 1800's to the now deceased owner, from his girlfriend expressing her feelings in having to leave him because of the death of her mother in another town. He burned to death before her return.

Another cook who once worked at the hotel told us, "I was working alone in the kitchen one night, when the freezer door, which was locked, flung open. When I turned around, I noticed that the garbage had been moved. I yelled out because I thought someone was playing a joke on me, but indeed, the building was empty. When I turned around to return to the kitchen, I saw a man standing there. I said, 'Okay, enough is enough!' but then he disappeared. I ran from the building."

Several other bone chilling incidents have taken place around this person while working in the Georgetown Hotel. Twice in one week she remembered locking the door upon leaving for the night, and was puzzled to find it wide open when she returned the next morning. Nothing was missing from the premises. Another time she went to empty the trash and was locked out from the side entrance. She had to go around to the front door. She soon found more hospitable employment.

But upstairs the ghost prefers to stay in the room that was room 13. Guests who have occupied that room complained of "weird and strange noises, bumps and crashes in the night." One woman complained of someone, or something, that was invisible sitting on her feet. "They were frozen," she said. "There was enough pressure for perhaps a small dog, or animal, to have sat down on them. After much shuffling of my legs, I was finally able to fling it off."

"Another strange thing happened a few winters ago," stated Jack White, Thompson's business partner when interviewed in 1983. He looked up thoughtfully. "Bobbie and I heard something at the front door. It had snowed the night before, and the drifts against the door were at least two feet high. We wondered who could have made their way up to it. When we opened the door, we were astounded! We found deer tracks coming up to the door, but there was no deer. Stranger still, there were no deer tracks going the other way showing that he had turned around and left! It was as if the deer come up to the door and disappeared into thin air! Now, what do you think of that?" he asked, as if wanting an explanation. I offered that perhaps the phantom deer did not go around, but right through the bolted door and was residing inside the hotel. There are no barriers such as walls or doors on the 'other side'.

In the past, and in this rambunctious hotel, rumor had it a man shot himself through the foot at the bar, an angry boyfriend shot his girlfriend through the hip in a jealous rage, and many in the bar have clapped their hands approvingly at the clanging bell which was suspended by a string at the ceiling, attached to a bed upstairs destined to go off each time the bed moves. Often called the "Honeymoon Room," the occupants would more times than not come down the stairs to a round of applause from the bar-hops. But none of these events, true or not, could be as exciting as the sightings of the tall dark ghost of the Georgetown Hotel. These haunted hills do have their secrets. For those of you who believe, and those of you that don't, our suggestion is to be aware this Halloween if you pass the Georgetown Hotel and see someone in costume not asking for tricks or treats. You just might have encountered the Georgetown Hotel Ghost!

NOTE: THE Georgetown Hotel and Bar is located at:
                6260 Main Street
                Georgetown, CA. 95634
                (530) 333-2848

AMERICAN RIVER INN
Where Yesterday's Lovers Still Reside

No story about ghosts and love would be complete without mentioning the American River Inn. Nor would it be complete without the tale of hospitality and loneliness. The two go hand in hand. It's the Romeo and Juliet for all ages, and it happened right here in Georgetown.

A gruff old miner haunts Room 5 of the beautiful American River Inn in downtown Georgetown. He abruptly makes his presence known on a whim, yet despite his disheveled appearance, he rarely has a frightening effect on the guests. He is a man of tender

101

nature, regardless of his adverse appearance. And he loves three things, honeymooners or happy lovers, Room 5 of the Inn, and his long-dead girlfriend, for whom he is still pining. Rumor tells us he last saw her in Room 5.

During the Gold Rush days, the American River Inn was known as the American Hotel (circa 1853). There were a series of owners, name changes, and rebuildings required courtesy of the fires that caused widespread havoc through Georgetown. The American Hotel was constructed over a productive lode known as the Woodside Mine. From the Woodside Mine, many pound-sized chunks found their way into miners hands. At one point as much as $90,000 was pulled from the earth within two weeks. Then, as if in retribution for the gold taken from their ground, the mine painfully claimed the lives of many of the hard working men trapped within their confines. The grounds slowly sucked the air out of them, but did not spit them out. Some are believed to still be buried under the American River Inn, from when that mine collapsed. Taking a walk downstairs, a basement wall hides the grim story. Oscar survived that catastrophe. Such begins the tale of Oscar, our honeymoon ghost.

He was a hearty soul of the 1800's, a miner looking for fortune like thousands of others at this time in history. He must have made an impact on the townsfolk, as his name is synonymous with Georgetown even to this day. Old timers tell tales about Oscar. He is remembered by stories passed down through generations as a gruffy old poke, about 5'8", ambitious and anxious to find his fortune. If there was a strike, Oscar was the first to pick up a shovel. He was fearless in the rickety mine shafts, and

102

tapped off river channels. Once known to be lost for several days in an extensively channeled abandoned mine, he emerged complaining he "Didn't find no gold!" The cheering of the crowd that had been diligently looking for him came to a complete stop. "Now lets get back in the mine!" he told his surprised friends. Such was his self-programmed thinking. Or did he have a special need for the gold. He had a perpetual romantic heart, and was to give his, foolishly or not, to a nameless 'woman of the evening.'

Now there was a time our beautiful American River Inn was not as luxurious as it is today, and a time when it was used for other types of guests than those the management caters to now. As we said before, miners had needs and in Georgetown they were often met at the American Hotel. As the tale goes, Oscar fell hard for a Gold Rush prostitute. He was well aware of her occupation, in fact, it was how they met. Many years her senior, he was smitten enough to dream of making her his wife. They had long talks, before and after lovemaking. She told of missing her family in the east, and of making enough money to return there.

Whether the story is true, or if it is all conjecture, we cannot know for certain, but the ghost of the American River Inn certainly takes on all appearances and characteristics of the seemingly immortal Oscar. And, because we all have to die, Oscar found his demise suddenly one day, just above the Woodside Mine he once worked.

When not searching for elusive metal, he had taken a job as a carpenter on the property, to be near his love. History shows he was very jealous of her. A heckler, a former 'client' of his girlfriend, insisted on belittling her name.

Words were passed between the men. A scuffle prevailed, and in the heated moments that followed, the aggressor shot Oscar dead, on the steps of the American Hotel. His body died, but his spirit remained.

"The activity seems to be centered around the top of the stairs, and Room 5," stated Carol La Morte, who along with her husband Neal and owners Wil and Maria Collin purchased the American Hotel in 1984 as a family project, and embarked on the biggest challenge of their lives. They renamed the hotel the American River Inn, and for three long and painful months remodeled, added eight bathrooms, reconstructed old woodwork and paneling, chose wallpaper reminiscent of the gold Rush era, and all in all, changed a declining fortress into a stately mansion. "Room 5 was in especially bad shape" she was to tell Gold Rush Ghosts, and which was evident from the photographs of before and after she was eager to show us. "Besides the bad shape, we began to feel uncomfortable working in the room. We were cold on a hot day. Something would brush past us, we could physically feel it, but no one was there. There was a 'presence' in that room as we worked it, but because the other members of our family did not want to admit to a 'ghost' I tried to concentrate on other aspects of what it could be. Obviously, since we have been admitting guests into that room for overnight stay, and they have actually seen a ghost, we have got to admit that he is here. And, whats interesting, is that very few of our guests are terrified of him, though he is gruff looking. He is a friendly ghost, who smiles at the lovers, and walks through the room as if he belongs there. He especially takes pride in appearing to honeymoon guests, as if he wants to be a part of their happiness."

Guests bear this out.   A statesman who wishes to remain anonymous told the author, "When we married, my wife and I stayed in Room 5 of the Inn.   At 3:00 a.m., a man dressed in old, tattered clothes walked through the closed door that leads to the hall. Our light switched on for no reason, and he smiled as he continued walking through the closed door that leads to the hall. We both heard his footsteps seemingly go down the stairs to the main part of the house, but I must admit neither of us got out of bed to check this out. Our light then went back off.   When I turned the light knob, it went back on because the lamp had been turned off the whole time."   La Morte admits to us, and through affidavits, that electricians have been called to fix the problem, but to no avail.   They now shrug their shoulders and say there is no possible electrical reason for this annoying fiasco.

The guest book at the American River Inn makes interesting reading. One couple, from Crestline California, wrote "We loved the experiencing the comfort and romance of your beautiful Inn. Pam enjoyed feeling Oscar in our room and maybe she'll be able to sleep at our next stop."   Another guest enthusiastically wrote: "We have already made reservations for next time.   Long 'live' Oscar!"   In November a couple from Yuba City, California wrote: "The highlight of our visit was a visit from Oscar. In the wee hours our lamp went on for no reason. We're sure it was Oscar!"

Help at the Inn often experiences his presence when cleaning the room. La Morte admits to "talking to him when I know he is around so I won't get afraid."   Several guests have told the management, "We were snug in our bed when this dirty looking miner type walked into the room, smiled at us, and left through the door." Oscar always enters through the door that opens up on the balcony, and leaves through the door at the top of the stairs. It makes no difference if the door is open or shut, he does not take time to fiddle with it.

"And, he has an uncanny way of whispering your name," La Morte was to admit to us. "Several guests complained of hearing their names spoken and no one was there." A letter received by the Inn written by guests from Hawaiian Gardens, CA. states in part, "That evening at cheese and wine my husband and I were talking to each other. We learned that both of us felt uncomfortable each time we passed a specific part of the house. We compared notes and came to the conclusion that this is (must be) the house. I would appreciate any information....."

The beautiful American River Inn holds the secret of the graggy miner and his woman of the evening. Their never ending passion continues, as as he roams the halls in search of his love.

During a stay on June 23, 1986, a couple from Garden Valley, CA. told of hearing a woman's voice as well as a man's in Room 5 of the Inn. Because it was not publicized, the ghost in the building was somewhat a secret. None of the guests had prior knowledge that anything should be different about their stay. "We had just built our home and were celebrating by staying in the elegant Inn," the husband, a maintenance supervisor for the Roads Department of El Dorado County told the author. "In the middle of the night I awoke to a whisper near my pillow. When I sat up, it was gone. Figuring I was just dreaming, I laid my head back down. Immediately the whisper was back. I heard a man in the background, but though I could not quite make out what they were saying, it was a woman's voice I heard distinctly. Then, I heard footsteps going down the stairs. The American River Inn is a great place, and I had one of the oddest experiences of my life in Room 5. I will never forget it."

All guests want to come back to the American Inn. The management is so friendly and contented, it is obvious there is nothing here to fear. Everyone hopes for a chance to see Oscar.

But because a woman's voice is also sometimes heard from the depths of the unknown inside the Inn, it is interesting to note that soon after Oscar's death, a beautiful woman of the evening was to attire herself in her finest negligee, and, liquor in hand, take the leap of death from the balcony of the American Hotel. The doctor said her neck was broken instantly. Could it be a broken heart preceded it?

NOTE: The American River Inn is located at:
      Main at Orleans Street
      Georgetown,CA. 95634
      (530) 333-4499
      (800) 245-6566

The American River Inn is a beautiful Bed
and Breakfast, with check in time at 3:00 to
6:00 PM. There is a mountain pool and spa
for your enjoyment. Local wines are served
each evening in their parlor. The American
River Inn provides elegant wedding and
meeting facilities.

7

AMADOR CITY
Two Very Haunted Places To Visit

The town of Amador City, which incorporates both the Mine House Inn and the Imperial Hotel, is situated between Drytown and Sutter Creek on Hwy 49. Named for a miner, Jose M. Amador about the time the country separated from Calaveras County in 1854, the first discovery of gold was made soon after in one of the towns rich quartz mines. The glittering ore was discovered by a minister, and he must have been very blessed that day, as little gold was extracted from the area after that. Quartz mining went on to be a prosperous concern however, and supported the men who worked the mines, usually quite handsomely. Remnants of the largest mine, the Keystone, still overlooks the town from the south end of the county.

MINE HOUSE INN
Mighty Beautiful, But Keep It Clean!

Come up the pathway, clean your shoes, and watch a serious looking old woman scold her alcoholic husband. In fact, she's so angry at him she locks him out of the house. He's long dead, and invisible to us, but she obviously does not know he is gone. The woman apparently has not figured out that she was supposed to go on to her 'final reward' many years ago too. She is happy to see company, however, and never gets in your way. Unless you leave a mess!

In 1868, this beautiful brick Victorian building was completed. It was constructed to house the offices of one of the highest gold yielding businesses in Amador County, the Keystone Mine. So rich was this find, no expense was spared in its development. When completed, a party was held for employees, officials, and townspeople. Eight well equipped rooms were displayed proudly, for from this imposing structure all fazes of the gold business could be conducted. And so it would be for many years.

But leaping forward to 1993. The Mine is no longer in service, and the beautiful building in disarray. A part of history rusting and needing care. What a shame!

"We couldn't just let it sit there!" Stated Rose Mendy when she talked to us about her Mine House. "It was so interesting, sitting up on the hill overlooking everything. And the grounds were so perfect for landscaping. Just what I always wanted. It had 200 year old oak trees, one just behind the upstairs rooms, on the hill. We couldn't resist!"

Both Engineers in the Bay area, Rose and her husband Allen wanted to do something new and to get away from the city. They researched and looked around the country for 'just the right thing.' Nothing was quite right until Rose saw the Mine House. She knew immediately that this was HER place. "The building had it's first remodel in

1957, but it was in real need" she told us.
"I just closed my eyes and started to do!"
With painstaking detail, the couple
restored, and reinstated, bringing the
structure back to it's original Victorian
glory. Then they went about meticulously
decorating the rooms, with Rose's flair for
color, adding to its authentic furniture and
accessories of the era. On occasion they
sat back and looked at when they had done.
They were happy with their Mine House. And
then they realized they got something in the
deal their money could not buy, and they
certainly had not expected in the purchase
price. They got ghosts!

"I first noticed something being strange
when I was in one of the downstairs
bedrooms" Rose told us. "I would hear
footsteps going around the building. On
the other side of the house, my mother, in
the kitchen area, would hear them too. We
both walked toward the footsteps thinking to
greet an early guest. Imagine our surprise
when we met each other on the path. We
were both unnerved because there was no one
there but us. There was no place the
person making the footsteps could have left
the path and moved out of sight. There was
just no one there." She thought about it
for a moment. "When things like this
continued to happen, we had to agree that
something strange was going on. Could it
be from another dimension? What other
explanation could there be?"

Things did not stop there. "Soon we
noticed there were times that the water in
the sinks of the bedrooms would be on when
no one was in the rooms. This seemed to
follow a pattern. Whenever we had a guest
in our Inn that was a little sloppy, the
water would be running after they left. It
seemed our ghost did not like things dirty

or out of order."

Rumor has it, in the 1800, there was a caretaker and his wife who lived on the premises. His job was to be certain no one was permitted on the grounds without authorization when the offices were closed, and the gold was locked up and safe. He was free with his booze, but this did not seem to interfere with his ability to do his job. His wife's duties were to occasionally cook for the men, clean the offices, and oversee the general care of the building and grounds. Finicky in her appearance and work ethic, this stern but reliable woman ran the place with an iron hand. She hated her husbands sloppy habits and love of the bottle. She wished she had never married him. His meager salary, a place to live, and nowhere else to go were her incentives to accept her fate. She was given a lot of respect and kindness by the men who owned and worked the Mine, and she felt they appreciated her. Her one stronghold was her feeling of importance among the men. Degrading her husband whenever possible was an added plus.

"She sits in the upstairs bedroom, above the office" our psychic Rosie Dean was to tell us. "There she can see if her husband is coming up the path. She says her name is Sarah, and she can also look out the window and watch for new guests, or anyone else who might need her help. She has a large, fat, spoiled, white cat at her side. She lavishes affection on this pet." The animal rubbed against Rosie's leg, then jumped up on to a chair.

"There is also a young girl who likes the Director's Room" Pat Kenyon was to tell us. "She was injured outside the building and brought here for a doctor to look at. I believe she was the victim of a stampeding horse. I do not know if she died in this room, but she is comfortable here and is wanting to stay. It is warm and comfortable. She wears a white pinafore type dress and black button shoes. She is delightfully impish, and will tease Sarah's cat, which causes all kinds of a fuss. She also likes to take the beds apart, especially when she is bored. Making a bed in this room can be an all day job if she feels like being ornery."

The owners of the Inn have left the original names on all the rooms. In the Mill Grinding Room you can still see the shaft which supports the wood ceiling which held the grinding wheels. They were used to pulverize the core samples prior to assaying. The Assay Room's display case contain original artifacts from the mining era. The Vault Room contains the original Keystone Mine safe where gold bullion was stored before being loaded on Wells Fargo Stagecoaches for it's trip to San Francisco. Also beautiful are the Stores Room, the Directors Room, the Bookkeeping Room and the Retort Room, where gold was smelted, and the newest, added about 1915, the Keystone Room. The Inn is conveniently located on highway 49, about 2 miles from Sutter Creek, another well haunted Gold Rush town, and about a 45 mile drive from Sacramento.

The owners and innkeepers live in the superintendents home, also on the property and which is next to the Mine House. After our departure the owners told us their lights went off and on for no reason in their old residence. "We found this unnerving" Rose was to tell us. "Maybe we should have had you come over here too. We apparently have a ghost in this place as well."

To do in the area are fishing, skiing,

gold-panning, antique shopping, wine tasting, hiking, and golfing. But we suggest you spend your days and evenings enjoying the Inn and grounds. The ghosts are an added bonus!

NOTE: The Mine House Inn is located at:
        14125 State Highway 49
        Amador City,CA. 95601
        (209)267-5900

Wake up at the Mine House Inn and ring for a hearty breakfast served directly to your room. A heated pool is provided for your enjoyment. Some rooms have their own fireplaces.

Beautiful, but one ghost insists you keep it clean or, she will!

IMPERIAL HOTEL
The Ghost on the Wall

Elwin Harris Jacobson flagged down the hurried waitress. "Could you please get us a glass of water" he asked her? He and his wife had just returned from a long day of antique shopping in Amador City and nearby Sutter Creek. His wife, in fragile health, was parched and exhausted. Blaming himself for keeping her out in the sun so long, and not meaning to appear rude or impatient to the floorperson, he added, "I would really appreciate it!" The hostess did not alter her steps as she rushed by, but raised her fingers to indicate did he want two glasses? "Yes" he told her, and added "Thank you."

A few minutes later a server came to the table. Bringing a menu, she asked if she could get the couple something to drink.

"Oh, why, no, thank you" Jacobson told her, confused. "I think the hostess is bringing us water" he explained.

The server looked around the room, questioningly. She shrugged her shoulders. "Well, I don't know who that could be" the puzzled waitress told him. "I am the only server in the dining area right now, in fact, someone called in sick so we are short handed." She smiled at the pleasant couple. "Well, whoever it is, I certainly appreciate any help I can get!" They laughed as she thought the bartender or someone from the kitchen had perhaps been summoned to assist. Upon checking, and then waiting for the elusive glasses of water which never showed up at their table, the couple and the server passed the mystery off as just one of those unexplainable things that happens to all of us at one time or another. The waitress then brought the

Jacobson's their water, and soon their dinner selection, as the incident was forgotten in the contentment on an enjoyable meal and friendly company. It was only later that the couple were to reminisce about the dress of the unidentified, mysterious, and non-returning hostess. "She looked like she was wearing a dress similar to the dress the women in that painting on the wall is wearing" Jacobson was to point out to his wife. "And her facial features look the same."

"Well I believe it was the women in the picture" his wife answered more certain than her husband, having studied the face of the passing hostess more closely as women often do. "Why don't we ask the waitress who the woman in the painting is?"

The Imperial Hotel's brick building was originally built in 1879 to function as a mercantile store to provide for the needs of the homeless miners. Realizing the town was inundated with stores, and its profit margin almost nil, the owner/builder, B. Sanguinetti saw a better opportunity to pay his bills and aid the ever increasing population. He renovated his building as a hotel and boarding house. His instincts correct, the new business prospered. So well, in fact, the following year a two story addition was needed to further accommodate his clientele. But years would pass, and people would die, as others born, and weather and time took their inevitable toll on everything in sight. A remodel began in 1968, and revisions continued thru the seventies, as the building served as spaces for shops, a hotel, rooms for rent, and a mini-mall.

In 1988, so many years later, the two current innkeepers, who are also the owners of the stately building, had an idea.

Adventurous in nature and with love for a new project, they undertook the challenge of their lives as they made a decision to restore the old building.

"Its then that strange things started happening around here" Bruce Sherrill was to tell the author. "My partner Dale Martin and I worked endlessly to bring the building back to it's original prominence, but every so often it seemed like someone was looking over our shoulders. Sometimes it seemed like jobs would take longer than we anticipated. Sometimes tools would be misplaced." He smiled at us. "Who can explain it?"

About six years ago, the owners decided to enjoy a holiday. Not wanting to leave the building unattended at night, they asked the assistance of Dale's sister, Treva Burke, and her husband who lived just across the street. The couple agreed to oversee the operation, and to check for any disturbances at night. Secure they had covered all possibilities, Bruce and Dale left for their vacation. In the middle of the night a light came on in the upstairs quarters of the unoccupied Imperial Hotel. Treva bravely left her home and in the eerie darkness, crossed the street to carefully unlock the clearly secured door to the building. She slowly climbed the stairs, and looking over her shoulder, turned it off. We are certain she exited the Imperial Hotel quickly to return to the sanctuary of her own warm home.

"There is also the incident of our friends from Washington" Bruce was to remember. "It happened about three years ago. One evening while visiting us at the hotel, they left their room to get something to eat. It was dark and they said they were fumbling for the light switch. Just as they were about to reach around the corner and flick the light on, it came on by itself. You can imagine how unnerving that must have been!"

And so it would for anyone. There have been many rumors circulating concerning the ghosts in the building. Many from as far back as the 1800's. Ghosts have been seen walking the halls, and enjoying the scenery. While <u>Gold</u> <u>Rush</u> <u>Ghosts</u> was investigating the building, Bruce was shocked to fine one of the bedrooms locked. "The room is not occupied, and there is no reason for this" he told us. As he opened the door to let us in, the fan came on by itself. Proof enough for this author and one of her photographers.

The kitchen has also been a great place for phenomena, as well as the basement. Recently, a dishwasher, the last one to leave the building for the night, heard footsteps in the basement and also upstairs while cleaning up. "The noise sounded like someone dragging something behind him."
The employee hurriedly exited the building, forgetting to lock up for the night. He never returned for his jacket.

But they are friendly ghosts, and the building is loaded with charm, as is Bruce. We have not as yet had the pleasure of meeting Dale, but we intend to. This is one place we will visit again. The dining area is beautiful, the food excellent, the lounge lovely in that old fashioned warm way. The rooms will overtake you, with their own character, each and every one. Artist John Johannsen, formerly from San Francisco, and who now operates from his studio in Jackson, California, has whimsically painted the rooms with surprises not found elsewhere.

Great food, great company, and the mysterous
lady on the wall.

Could the woman in the painting on the
wall be one of the ghosts that haunt the
Imperial Hotel? The waitress didn't know.
And we don't know. The picture was given
to Bruce and Dale by their artist friend

119

John Johannsen, and they believe it originally came from San Francisco. Where did he get it, did he paint it, and was it a person, long ago, associated with the Imperial Hotel? You would have to ask Bruce and Dale. Or visit The Johannsen gallery for the answer to that one. Ah mysteries! They are what makes the world go around.

NOTE: The Imperial Hotel is located at:
        14202 State Hwy 49
        Amador City, CA. 95601
        (800) 242-5594
The Imperial Hotel invites you to call, or just stop by. The restaurant is open every day from 5 to 9 P.M. Brunch is served Sundays from 10 a.m. to 2 p.m. February thru October.
The Imperial Hotel arranges group luncheons, weddings to die for, and special parties. The Imperial Hotel lists a full bar, with special desserts and pastries. Patio dining is also available.

8.

SUTTER CREEK
Antiques, Boardwalks and a Walk Into
Yesterday

Sutter Creek, just three miles north of Amador City, is a delight to see. The town was named for our illustrious John Sutter, as he came to mine the area after his other endeavors failed. He brought with him a group of Indians to help him find his gold. As with bad luck following him, miners already in the area took a complete dislike to him. Whether they feared he might 'jinx' the gold discovery, or if they were jealous of him, they made his life hell. Finally, for lack of another excuse, they accused him of slavery. The pressure too much, he left the area.

A former merchant of Sutter Creek had another type of luck. Leland Stanford could do no wrong. He purchased the Lincoln Mine, expecting to get rich. Just as he was about to give up, he found a rich vein. Color! His future assured he branched out to join three other entrepreneurs, Hopkins, Crocker, and Huntington to build the Central Pacific Railroad. Eventually Stanford became a U.S. Senator, and Governor of California. Stanford University? Yup! Leland Stanford, the founder.

So, taking the good luck with the bad luck, Sutter Creek has had as interesting

past as any in the Gold Rush country. And
about dusk, strange shadows sometimes appear
along the hillsides. Strange noises of
unidentified means are heard. Her old
buildings have secrets to tell. Here is the
story of the most remarkable one.

THE SUTTER CREEK INN
Jane Way's Wonderful House

"I will protect your Inn" a spirit told
Jane Way in 1966, soon after she purchased a
16-room New England style home in Sutter
Creek with hopes of creating a beautiful
Inn. And he kept his word. What he didn't
tell her, was with the package she would
find her life forever changed. She now
intermingles with guests from today, and
those from another time. The idea of an inn
apparently appealed greatly to her non-
paying guests. And Jane, one of the most
remarkable women you will ever meet, took it
in stride and has made her ghosts welcome.
It's a fair trade! The Sutter Creek Inn is
the proof. It is one of the most lovely and
enjoyable places to stay in all the Mother
Lode.
Approximately 32 miles from Placerville
on Hwy. 49, Sutter Creek will take your
breath away. Beautiful in it's well kept
stores and stately homes along the main
strip, the most magestic, and yet the one
that makes you feel most like home, is Jane
Way's Sutter Creek Inn. Quaint, nestled in
an instep of the High Sierras, the 1,200
foot elevated town is an artist's dream, a
panoramic view of old, well-kept homes, and
a boardwalk business area dotted with
antique shops. Everything takes us back to

the "olden days," probably not as it was, but as it should have been. Such is the way we found Sutter Creek.

We know the community was first named for John Sutter, our hero, whose gold find tipped the scale for populating the State. Ah, the rush for gold! Sutter Creek, however, did not come into being until sometime around 1851, when the before mentioned Leland Stanford was lucky enough to extract nearly one-half-million dollars in gold from a mine just outside what was then little more than a ramshackle town. Sutter Creek was to operate many mines during its day, including the last to operate in the Mother Lode, the Central Eureka, which closed its doors in 1959 after producing a whopping $25 million in gold.

But again we wander. The graceful white mansion, which is now Jane Way's Sutter Creek Inn, was first built in 1860 by John Keyes as a home for his beautiful young bride, Clara McIntyre. Longing for her native New Hampshire, Keyes fashioned the home in the popular New England style she was accustomed to. They appeared to be a bright and happy couple. It came as a sadness then, when they lost their only child to diphtheria while still a baby. There were to be no other children for the couple. Clara's fate was cast as she became a widow at thirty-four. Life was cruel then, as it sometimes is today.

Luckily for Clara, two years after her husband died, a dashing State Senator came to town. With all his finery, Edward Convers Voorhies proceeded to woo her. They were married on March 29, 1880, in her beautiful rose garden behind the house. The marriage appeared a happy one as well, and produced two children, Earl, who died in World War II, and Gertrude who lived to be ninety.

"I bought the house from Gertrude just before she moved to a rest home," Way explained.

"It was strange," Way told the author. "It was a rather unhappy time in my life. I purchased the Inn to get away from it all, and to make a complete change in my location and my life. I was, well, unsure."

Jane Way's enchanted cottage. The mansion has everything, including protective ghosts.

"The evening the ghost appeared, I had been invited to a costume party. I was getting dressed, when an eerie feeling of being watched enveloped me. I turned around and there, standing in the doorway, was a tall man in old-fashioned clothing. For a moment I thought he was going to the same party, but I remembered all of our guests were gone for the evening. It was then that I heard the words, "I will protect your Inn." He managed to smile at me as he faded away. Well, I should have been frightened, but I felt warm all over. I knew then that I had made the right decision. Someone from outside my world was taking an interest in my affairs. What more could I ask for?"

"It was later that I saw a photograph of Senator Edward Voorhies" she told us. "I recognized him immediately. I knew then that it was he who had visited me and said he was looking out for things." Later Ms. Way was to learn the Senator also had a home in the Homewood section of Lake Tahoe. To this day he is often seen there as well, at family functions and parties.

Gertrude Voorhies, the former owner, also visits the house. "She lived in this place all her life and loved it dearly," Way was to tell us. "She told me often before she died how attached she was to the home. My experiences with the continuity of life was enhanced soon after Gertrude's earthly death. One evening she appeared in the parlor. She seemed to be checking things out, looking around. She apparently loved this house so much that she just could not stay away. She just had to come back!"

"Another strange thing happened," Way told us, remembering. "My cat had just had kittens. She woke me in the middle of the night, and I suspected she was hungry.   I got out of bed, put on my robe, and followed her to the kitchen door. As we approached the entry, she bolted and arched, refusing to go in. I looked into the kitchen but no one was there. I could not get her to go in. I was annoyed at her strange behavior, and I tried to coax her with a little push, but she hissed and raised her claws at something unseen. I jumped back as in a flash, and without warning, her body was literally picked up out of thin air and flung across the room.

"The poor cat seemed stunned and frustrated, as surely she was, and so was I. My heart was pounding! But soon after that, the cat was willing to go into the kitchen as if nothing had happened, and eat her food. I later learned the original owner of the house hated cats!"

For all the ghosts, the Sutter Creek Inn remains one of the most popular resting spots in all of Northern California. Its rooms are booked weeks in advance, especially in the summer. "I guess that is because all of the ghosts are friendly," said Way. "At least to people."

"If you should see a ghost while you are here," Way advised us, "Tell them they are welcome and to make themselves comfortable". It is only fair. "They will make you feel that way!"

NOTE: The Sutter Creek Inn is located at:
75 Main Street
Sutter Creek,CA. 95685
(209) 267-5606
FAX (209) 267-9287

Guests at the Sutter Creek Inn may enjoy their excellent library, piano, and game tables. They boast many fireplaces and warm hospitality. Full country breakfasts and afternoon refreshments are served. Laid back and beautiful, enjoy the private patios, lush gardens, grape arbors and hammocks. Handwriting analysis and massages are available by appointment.

9

JACKSON
Just A Haunted Town

Jackson, with todays population of approximately 3,900 folks, is remembered mostly for it's two no longer operating hard-rock mines, the Kennedy and the Argonaut. Both were instrumental to Jackson's early economy. An interesting town, still lazy and laid back, it has many Gold Rush buildings to enjoy on Main Street, housing antique and other interesting businesses. Although many of the original buildings were destroyed by fire in 1862, in the same hardy tradition common in the Gold Rush days, was rebuilt. Jackson is a fun way to spend a day, and the National Hotel and Louisiana House are a must.

THE NATIONAL HOTEL
Mist, Maze, and Mystery

Long dead gold miners that frighten drivers along a Gold Rush lane. Spirits that appear to guests at Gold Rush inns. Cemeteries from a long gone era that house living spirits. Ghosts, entities, cold spots, and things flung across the room by unseen hands. We have confirmed them all in the gold rush country. Yes, ghosts are commonplace in Northern California. And it has more. It has the National Hotel.

Driving down the road the first thing you notice on the corner of Main and Water Streets, is the National Hotel. It draws you like a magnet. It has that wonderful look of the old west, and so you let your mind step back into yesterday. You want to forget you are in a car so you park it on the side. You check your imaginary gun and holster, adjust your Stetson, and click your boots. Even as you park your car you know you want to go inside. You expect a gunfight to erupt as you cross the street, or a wagon to cross your path.

Although the old west feeling is all around, when you enter you are more likely to be surprised by the beauty of the hotel. Not to say it does not look like an 1800's building, because it does, but alas, a beautiful 1800's one. The wood is speechless, you'll love the banisters, and the lobby (bar) area includes red velvet curtains. Wow, you are impressed, and interested. It certainly looks like it should be haunted!

To the right we see the Saloon. We have read it is authentic, a kerosene burning chandelier and original back bar that dates to 1862. For now we are intrigued by the staircase on the left. It has a maze, an ectoplasmic fog surrounding it, and as we approach, our psychic sees three entities.

The first is a young boy of about seven or eight, and he is attempting to slide down the banister. He says his name is Jeffrey. Trailing him is his sister, and she appears to be about three years old, and in a white pinafore type dress with black button up shoes. She is angry at him for taking such a large lead, as her tiny legs cannot keep up with him. She gets down on her butt and tries to exit the stairs that way, one at a time. She continues to yell at her brother. He ignores her. Some things have just not changed through time!.

But now it gets complicated. Behind them a beautiful women comes into view. She is dressed in 1800's attire, and certainly does not appear to be a shabby housekeeper or such. No, she is of wealth, and has the bearing to prove it. She wears a light turquoise, lavender dress, full at the shoulders and extended to the floor. She wears long white gloves, lace, and is carrying a fan. Her hat is round and enormous, with more lace, and feathers in the front. Big, long feathers. Her make-up is impeccable, and you admire her from a distance. She seems to pay no attention to the children before her, but passes them by as she disappears at the bottom of the stairs. Two names come to mind, Sarah and Milly. We don't know which is the girl child and which name belongs to the beautiful woman.

We are now aware of the children again. They appear in a mist. A companion has joined them. It is a little dog, tan, and playful. He (she) is fuzzy with short legs, a Terrier/Cocker cross perhaps, but has wire haired whiskers protrude in odd places on his face. It is barking at the kids and apparently belongs to them. At least since he died.

Our psychic then looses contact with this other world as loud talking is heard from the bar. These are living folks here to have a good time. We cannot any longer communicate with the children so we precede up the stairs to the second floor.

It is February, and it has been a rainy year. We know the National Hotel was originally built around 1849 above two springs, and was used as a trail stop for travelers. Miners panned the stream, and we can imagine them being accommodated when panning was good at the new hotel. And because it appears for some perverse reason that all hotels in the Gold Rush country had to burn down at least once, (An omen perhaps) this one did in 1862, along with almost everything else on Main Street. Learning a lesson, this time the stately building was rebuilt on a brick basement.

But take a walk up the stairs from the bar area and see the remains of generations past. Beautifully decorated with antiques and in the style of the 1800's early 1900's, you are now sure you have entered the world of days gone by. A quieter time perhaps, at least different. No cell phones, no rushing to the store before it closes, and no studying for exams. No, you are now a 49er, and at the National Hotel.

"Sarah......Sarah......" a voice breaks into the air. "Wait!" Another beautiful spirit woman, this one a bit stockier but dressed as well. We now know the lovely entity on the stairs was Sarah and the child Milly, as this woman is certainly trying to catch up with her friend in torquoise and lavender. She races through Dan, our photographer, unaware, and heads down the stairs. A party perhaps? We wish we had been invited! We feel these lovely rooms were once used for ladies of the evening, a bordello, but this is not our experience now. We know for certain the miners were accommodated, and what more beautiful place but here. We have tapped into another time, the aura of wealth and stature. There is the feeling of splendor, the best there is. It is common knowledge the elite of the gold rush days stayed at the National Hotel.

Every governor of California since 1861 has been a guest. Which are here now? And get those kids off the steps!

It is entertaining, but lonely. Not one living person, or one from the past, is now on the second floor. We assume they have all gone somewhere together, because empty wine glasses are left around. A man's silk scarf is thrown over a chair, forgotten in the rush, and we assume they have all gone to the function that has claimed both ladies. We decide to precede to the third floor, see if things are livelier there. We climb the stairs with hope. Ah, much better. From a door on the third floor we watch the raging water below us. It is February, and it has been a rainy year. And, indeed, there is much ghostly activity here.

"I am having trouble breathing" our psychic tells us. "I believe there was an epidemic at one time. Influenza, diphtheria. There were many people here, suffering. Fever. Trying to get well. I see nurses, doctors. "They are all gone now" we are assured, we just tapped into the energy of things before. Remember, these were the days before penicillin and other wonder drugs. The sick were usually kept on the same floor and away from the children and healthy. This period extended for months" we were told by our psychic. "But the rooms are much more accommodating now. I see men from the river coming directly from their work to this floor. I see a cat, living on this floor who belongs to everyone. Names of some who still abound are George, Harry and Otis. There is a Dennis, from New England, a young boy, perhaps about 18. He says he finds this life hard and wants to go back to the east. The others keep watch of him, let him hang

131

around with them.   They are friendly, and happy to have company.   They are playing cards, and we hear them bragging about their luck, not one telling the truth.   Much as we find this entertaining, we decide to go back downstairs. We wonder if anyone at the bar has had an experience with the ghosts at the National Hotel.

Spirits of the past abound.   Especially the beautiful lady, and the children on the stairs.

"I have" states Anthony Matranga, a carpenter who has worked on the building for the last four years. "I told you guys this place was haunted!" he says to his buddies. "All of us find strange things happening when we are here."

He is anxious to tell his story.   "In the summer of 1997, I stayed overnight on the third floor.   I had been working on the building and it was simpler than going home. I had finished my work for the evening, and admit to having a few cocktails, but certainly I was not drunk.

"As I approached my room, my heart hurt. I had trouble breathing. It felt like something had reached out and grabbed my chest. Uncomfortable as it was, it soon went away. I didn't give it much more thought except the feeling was gone and I was glad for that. I slipped off my shoes and got into bed.

Then I heard footsteps in the hall. A lady with an Irish accent started talking in the next room. I knew this could not be happening because we were under construction, and this section was closed off. I knew I was the only person on the floor. Then another strange thing happened. I could see lights under my bedroom door, coming from the hall. This was certainly impossible because I had the power turned off at the box. I started to get up and fumble for my shoes. Then, in the room on the other side of mine, water started to run. It continued for a long time, and then, someone walked over to the bed because I could hear them lay down. The bed springs began to make noise and I knew what was going on. For just a moment I felt jealous because I was here alone!

Of course there was no one there. Spooky as it was, this sort of thing is becoming common place around here.

Nancy Banducci one of the owners of the hotel told the author, "My office is across from one of the rest rooms. A guest had gone into the restroom and I had gone into the office. We both heard a loud crash, as if glass was being broken. I immediately thought of irreplaceable antiques in a hutch. Running from both rooms, the woman and I met in the hall. We both hunted the complete building but nothing was amiss. No broken glass. And yet we both heard it

133

distinctly.

This lovely hotel has 30 available rooms that range from double to queen size beds. John "Duke" Wayne has stayed here, as well as director John Ford. Presidents Garfield and Hoover have signed the register, as well as Will Rogers and Paul of Yugoslavia. It is believed "Black Bart" was also a guest.

The National Hotel does hold her mysteries. Things can be left at one place and found in another. People can be spoken to that are not there. An older man, stocky and balding may meet you at the front door and bow as you enter. You smile at him but he is gone.

Mist, mazes and mysteries. Maybe you will be the next one to tell us your experience.

NOTE: The National Hotel is located at:
2 Water Street
Jackson, CA. 95642
(209)-223-0500

Entertainment is available on Friday, Saturday and Sunday. On special occasions the National Hotel offers Dixieland bands, Blue grass, Banjo, and German Accordion polka. The hotel features daily prepared seasonal dishes, and an extended library and big screen T.V. is available for adults and children. A scent of lilac is often in the air from days gone by, courtesy of the unknown. The National Hotel is available for banquets upon request.

Established in 1862-and the doors haven't been locked since!

10.

IONE

During the Gold Rush days it is said the Sacramento stage route, passing through several small towns including Ione, carried more than $270 million in gold bullion. One of these stops was made at the Q. Ranch, to the northwest of Ione. Ione, however, has not gone down in history as a mining camp, but as an agricultural metropolis. Strategically located 40 miles east of Sacramento on hwy. 104, it is easy to find and worth the trip.

During it's camp days, Ione was nicknamed Bedbug and then Freezeout. Perhaps imaginative, but embarrassing in its implication. Townsfolk soon settled on Ione. A good idea. Ione is clean and pretty and fun and entertaining. The Q. Ranch of yesterday is long gone, but this town still has her ghosts. Here are the stories of two of the most credible ones.

THE IONE HOTEL

Gregarious George and His Friends

A man staggers into room 13. He is not very tall, a bit stocky, and what remaining hair he has is gray around the edges. He looks annoyed as he pulls the covers from your bed. His voice is a deep harsh sound "You cannot sleep here" he tells you bluntly.

It is the middle of the night and you are annoyed. You had made a reservation and then paid in full for this room. Not to be intimidated you pull the remaining sheet up over yourself and yell at him to get out of your room. He looks at your husband lying beside you, and picks up an imaginary water pitcher, walks to the other side of the bed, and pours the invisible water on your companion. With a mischevious smirk he opens the door and you can see out into the hall. Your husband, awake now, jumps out of bed to follow the man only to crash into the door. It is still locked from the inside.

Welcome to Room 13. You have just had an unofficial visit from Gregarious George, one of the strongest spirit of the Ione Hotel. In his defense, he just wants you out of his room. He's harboring a hangover and needs the bed. Circumstances being different he probably would let you stay.

Ah George! Those who knew him insist he was friendly and outgoing. After work each day he would scout the local bars to drink with his friends, and eventually land up with a nightcap at the hotel. Unfortunately, back in those days, if one of his intoxicated friends was sloshed before him, they would "borrow" his room until he came home. George would come up the stairs, enter his room, at which time he would remove the covers, and drop them to the floor. After all, an inebriated man in need of his bed does not have much tact. George died here at the hotel, and still stays around, because, well, it is much more pleasant than going home. Unless he has invited you in to play cards, he figures anyone in his room is just more folks taking advantage of his hospitality.

Ole' George is more gracious with women. More likely he would sleep down the hall. Women in Room 13 rarely have to worry about George. Unless you're with some guy.......

Milly Jones, a delightful yet no nonsense type of person purchased the hotel in 1977. Soon after she saw what appeared to be smoke in the dining room. She watched as the floating cloud formed into a pyramid shape. "My hair went up" she said, "And I couldn't imagine what it was?"

The cloud continued to float in the air, and refused to move from the same spot. Curious, she waited for it to dissipate, but it hovered in the same place. Walking over to it, she blew as hard as she could. The unknown smoke moved, broke up into small pieces, but then reformed and came back to the same place. It began to vibrate.

Milly called the teenage dishwasher to the room. "What is that?" she asked the boy.

"Well, it must be cigarette smoke or from the kitchen" he told her, not sure of either explanation.

"Well, there are no smokers in here, and nothing is burning in the kitchen" she said.

The boy took a wet dish towel and waved it into the pyramid. Again it scattered and then regrouped into the same shape and back to the same place.

Milly and the boy looked at each other neither wanting to be the first to say it. "GHOST!" They ran for the kitchen. From there they watched as the appendage slowly moved to the left side, shrunk, and as if sucked up through a vacuum, disappeared. This was to be the start of many encounters!

"We had strange 'gifts' come our way" Milly Jones shared with us. "One day a silk ladies shoelace appeared out of the blue and landed on the table. Another time a bartender saw something on the bar before opening in the morning. It was a grease cap from a Model T. Car." She smiled that infectious smile of hers. "We were always polite and said 'thank you' to whomever sent them to us."

She was also to relate she only had to ask for things and they would be appear for her. "Once we needed 72 steaks to get us through the week-end and the freezer was empty. The person in charge of ordering had forgot. We could not get a supplier to deliver at this late date. I said openly into the air' What will we do, we need those steaks'! Next time we opened the freezer, the steaks were there. I was never billed for them."

Another time she saw six clear, but fluted, carnival glass bowls in the cupboard and really wished she could have them. "I asked the previous owner if she wanted to take them with her, but she said 'no, use them to put ice cream in'. I was delighted that she had been gracious enough to give them to me, but I quietly dreamed of having a complete set. Again I left the thought in the air, and soon each time I opened the cupboard there was another dish. They seemed to come from everywhere, and nowhere" she was to share with us. "At the end of our ownership we had 30 plates."

The Ione Hotel is a nineteen century Golden Star hotel, restaurant and bar. Originally built in the early 1850's, there are 14 antique guest rooms, a balcony overlooking the age old Main Street, and another balcony from which you can see Sutter Creek. Beseeched with fires that plagued most buildings in the Gold Rush days, it survived and was rebuilt, to it's former speculations.

But this century as well, the Ione Hotel was destroyed by fire. In 1988, just as new owners Tom and Dorothy Shone purchased the building, it was again destroyed. As you meet the Shone's you recognize the determination to recreate. With painstaking back-breaking work they began the rebuild, making the structure even more beautiful. After almost 2 years of extensive renovation, they must have stopped momentarily to look at what they had done. What a job! Salvaging all they could from the original hotel, they rebuilt and then furnished with antiques and special touches to make your stay a luxurious step back into yesteryear, yet with the amenities of convenience which more than provide for creature comfort.

We first met Tom and Dorothy in February of 1998. She is one of those friendly and beautiful women that do not require make-up that are the envy of the rest of us. Tom has that great sense of humor that puts you at ease. They graciously allowed us into their world on a busy day, which most are at the Ione Hotel. Upon approaching the top of the stairs, our psychic Rosemary Dean was drawn to room 6. "Can we go into this room?" she asked. Dorothy unlocked the door and Rosie immediately felt the room had suffered a fire. Pat Kenyon felt the result. "A mother is telling me her child died here" she told us.

Having already heard the story, I confirmed this for her and asked what else she found. "Well, the child is not here, but as I said, the mother is" she said! and she is distraught ." Rosie than added, "And an older woman as well, I believe a grandmother, and I see a man coming in to help."

"It was not a hotel fire" Pat then told us, "but a room fire. The baby died of smoke inhalation in 1884. There was an older child as well" she told us, "I do not know if he was from this time frame but he comes in at this room. He was not hurt in the fire. There was no hotel fire this time."

The incident in question happened in the year 1884, which was not one of the years the hotel burned. This would then substantiate the fact that it would have had to be a room fire.

Gregarious George, his bar friends and card playing phantoms. Join the game, but don't sleep in his bed!

Milly Jones related this story to Gold Rush Ghosts on the phone one evening. She was being taught automatic writing by a psychic who insisted she try it in the company of friends, and an impartial person Milly had brought in from outside the building. Soon her arms became rigid; she could not drop the pen she was being forced to write the name Mary Phelps. The unseen entity also wrote about a child that she had lost in a fire. "It was an incredible time"

Jones was to relate to us.

Not to long after that a party of eight people came in to the restaurant. The waitress came back into the kitchen to get Milly. "A woman in the dining room insists on talking to you" she told her.

Wiping her hands on her apron, Jones went to the table. The wife's husband excused himself and headed to the bar. His wife slowly explained her story.

"I understand you have identified a Mary Phelps as being an entity in the hotel" she said, ruefully. "I thought you might want to know that my grandmother's name was Mary Phelps, and she and my great-grandmother stayed at the hotel. The woman returned the next day with her children and grandchildren. And a priest.

Another time Milly Jones watched as an elderly gentleman come in the front door. He walked directly toward her and she felt there was something not quite 'right' about him. She asked if she could get him a table at the restaurant but he continued to walk up to her. Getting into her space, she began to back up. "Restroom? Phone?" she asked, but he did not respond. He just kept coming forward.

Realizing she was about to bump up against the wall she put her hand on the old man's shoulder. Her hand did not stop on his shoulder but went right through his body to his back. She stepped aside as employees and patrons watched and let him pass. "He had been dead a long time" she said, because he had a distinct unpleasant odor."

News of the ghosts at the Ione Hotel spread throughout the country. Ripley's Believe It Or Not has been a guest. The show That's Incredible featured the Ione Hotel for it's viewers. Patrons of the restaurant, bar and hotel were delighted to tell their stories. The television crew soon learned to cover their equipment ("We offered bedspreads" Milly said) because the spirits are attached to lights, dials and switches and they would re-set or turn off the equipment.

There were thoughts that things might settle down after the 1988 fire and the change of ownership. Not a chance! A truck of building supplies arrived, mahogany, wood to be stacked and beams. Tom went across the empty yard to help the driver unload. Grabbing one end of several 2X4s, he headed to where he intended to stack them, again in the empty yard. In front of him he was startled to see a 6X8 beam clearly in his path. "How could that have gotten here from the time I walked toward the truck?" He knew no one had passed him. And then he remembered. No. It couldn't be the......!

Yup, they're still here. It soon became apparent to Tom and Dorothy that anything frilly or feminine hung in George's room was quickly knocked off the walls. After several guests related their stories, Tom & Dorothy decorated his room in a masculine motif. Appease him? It did, but he still wants people to know this is HIS room. Because of the many guests that have seen George in this room, Tom took count of how the rooms were numbered upstairs. He purposely added a room so he could make this his room No.# 13. A good choice!

"And then there is the story of the bartender" Dorothy and Tom told us. Not a believer in ghosts, he was surprised when the light went out for no reason. Then, it came back on. It could have stopped there, but something unseen touched his hand. He told our new friends he almost wet his pants!

The Ione Hotel is warm, charming and inviting, as are the Shones. They will graciously explain the rooms on the second floor, each carpeted, air conditioned, and with private bath. All rooms are elegantly decorated with antiques, many for sale. The rooms are easily accessible to front and rear balconies. Be sure to see the Bridal Suite, a personal favorite, with mahogany canopy bed, and Victorian bath. But remember, if you want a rugged, masculine room, and a ghost as well, visit room #13.

NOTE: The Ione Hotel is located at:
         25 W. Main
         Ione, CA. 95640
         (209) 274-6082
         Fax: (209) 274-0750

Lunch and Dinner are served daily. Breakfast service is available on Saturdays and Sundays, with Sunday Brunch served from 9:00 until 2:00. They provide banquet services, and catering to meet all party needs.

THE HEIRLOOM
Where Civil War is Remembered

Is he blue, or is he gray? He stands watch from the balcony of the lovely Heirloom Bed & Breakfast Inn in Ione, one hand over his heart. We know in Civil War days California was a neutral state, but he is just here for respite. He is a warrior, a soldier, and the uniform appears to be that of an officer. Is he comfortable here through time as a guest, or does he return to this precious home because it was his own? It is beautiful in its Victorian elegance with pillars, balconies, and brick that remind you without question of the better days from Gone With the Wind. With this in mind you think he must have fought for the South. He has been seen rolling small tobacco leaves into cigars, perhaps in what is known as a rope weave. You then remember a valuable lesson from school, tobacco was a big product, planted in the south. Yup, you are sure. Our phantom is a Confederate.

But then maybe no. His uniform appears dark in color, though the jacket is lighter than it should be, and you imagine it must just be faded from the many washings it has endured. He puts one of his boots up on a chair and shines it with a cloth. It is then you see the epaulets on his shoulders. Union epaulets, at least you think so. Ah mysteries, great mysteries.

Our Civil War soldier goes about his business without bothering the guests, and doesn't seem to care if you know he is a Yankee or a Reb. The war is over! Does he know it? Or is he unto himself, his world, perhaps in planning the next strategy or agonizing over the thought of having to go back to war.

But lets not speculate. Lets deal with the facts we know.

The Heirloom he loves was built around 1863 as a residence, with columns, two-storied gallery, french windows and fan transom. The brass plaque outside states the Heirloom is "An important local representative of the Greek revival tradition in America, the house, constructed of locally fired brick, served as a private residence for a number of Ione's prominent citizens. In 1980, it was converted into a bed and breakfast inn." It continues to let you know it was: "Dedicated by grand parlor native sons of the golden west, Walter G.Perazzo, Grand President March 10,1984 in memory of James D. Phelan, U.S.Senator."

144

The Heirloom surroundings are uncluttered by time. The long driveway takes you away from the busy streets and town noises to it's own quiet world. Our psychic Rosemary Dean immediately made contact with the soldier as we entered the second story of the Inn. He stood on the balcony but did not make conversation. Soon he walked away, into one of the beautiful bedrooms and looked out, as if to reflect. Obviously this one was HIS room, because he is familiar here. He took off his jacket and removed his saber, careful to hang it on the wall. He grabbed a book and sat down, ignoring our presence. And so we wandered.

Downstairs again, we were in awe of the beautiful antiques, a table just under the stairwell goes back 450 years! It is common knowledge that antique furniture can bring spirits with them as well, and so I asked our psychics, Rosie, and Pat Kenyon to only associate with those who are native to the building. We looked across the room at the beautiful age old piano. "It belonged to Lola Montez" Rosie told us, and this was confirmed. "She is not here however" the psychic apologized. Too bad. So many questions she could have answered.

"I have a Spanish women here" Pat was to tell us. "She is a housekeeper. I see her washing dishes and dusting furniture. I also see a black man, I believe he is a valet, a man's helper. In the field along the drive both Rosie and Pat saw a man working with metal tools. "I believe him to be a blacksmith, but more." Kenyon told us. "He makes farm tools, and repairs them. He works with metal, iron, and is real good at his work. He is harsh, or just too busy to communicate. A tree had recently been cut down at this side of the driveway. "I feel the spirit of someone having been buried here, near where the metal worker is" Rosie said. It was a grave at one time. There is a family plot, perhaps, on the premises but not here." She thought a moment. "This is a solitary grave, maybe one or two persons from the 1800's, but nothing sinister. They died natural deaths and were interred."

Back upstairs Kenyon saw the spirit of a young girl. "She is dressing for a party. I believe she stayed in this room quite often." Upon leaving she turned around to investigate herself in an imaginary mirror. "I believe she was a niece to the owner" Kenyon told us. "And a very pretty one."

Outside the Inn are two unique rooms if you really want privacy. They are called the Rooms For All Seasons and are in adobe (rammed earth joined cottages.)

But upstairs at the Heirloom there are four beautiful rooms for your enjoyment. The Springtime, with its yellow handmade quilt and private balcony, The Summer Room, sea foam and dusty rose motif, shaded by a 150 year old walnut tree, Autumn, with antique solid brass bed and semi-private balcony over looking the garden, and the Winter Room, with fireplace, handmade quilt, Colonial poster bed, and semi-private balcony.

You will love the innkeepers, Patricia Cross and Melisande Hubbs. Friendly and warm, they are happy to show you the beautiful antiques and explain about the ghosts. Especially the officer, because he seems to be around the most.

Recently a couple stayed at the Heirloom. They told the author: "It was midnight, and I woke up to see a Civil War gentleman in the room. I figured I must still be dreaming, so I pulled the covers off and sat up. Putting my feet on the floor, I turned around to where the man was, and he had not gone. I woke my wife and this must have annoyed him because he walked to the balcony and disappeared.

So here are your clues. We know he is an entity from the Civil War but not which side he fought on. We know his room is one with a balcony, and we know he is elusive as are the other spirits at the Heirloom Inn. We know he resides at the Heirloom, but would like to know why he wishes to stay. The rest is up to you. Perhaps you can solve the mystery of the Civil War Officer who insists on staying.

Note: The Heirloom is located at:
      214 Shakley Lane
      Ione, CA. 95640
      (209) 274-4468
      FAX (209) 274-0750

They feature a lovely romantic English garden. A complete French country breakfast is served in your room, or if you wish, on the veranda, the garden, or dining room. The Heirloom is ideal for receptions, parties, social gatherings, and business meetings. The innkeepers are happy to make arrangements for your special needs.

Beautiful mansion which houses the Civil War Ghost. Problem: Is he blue or is he Gray?

11.

MOKELUMNE HILL
Quaint, Quiet, and Questioning

If you are interested in visiting a small unassuming community of maybe 1,500 people, pretty much untouched by time, Mokelumne Hill is just what you are looking for. Nestled in what is considered the "Banana Belt" of the High Sierras, (Citrus has the audacity of growing here all year round to the dismay of other Northern California towns), the village boasts enchanting old homes and buildings that are colorful and well kept, grounds of lush foliage and beautiful trees, and a pioneer cemetery with it's curious old markers. All this offers you a lovely day of slow paced reminiscence. Not that Mokulmne Hill hasn't been plagued with it's own history of intense violence and retaliation. It is known that in one 17 week stretch, "Moc" Hill averaged at least one killin' a day during the Gold Rush. The Diggins were so rich that many claims were limited to 16 square feet. Tempers flared with suspected claim jumping continuous. Besides their other problems, the town had the distinction of being known to have two immigrant wars, the Chilean, and the French, just a few years later.

It seems that in a now vanished camp called Chili Gulch, there lived an unscrupulous Dr. Concha, who had a nasty habit of registering claims in the names of

148

his employees.   These workers were slaving
for him for less than meager earnings.   In
1849 the men got the courage to overthrow
him, unfortunately, at the loss of many
lives.   Thus the "Chilean War."   Different
circumstances perpetrated the "French War."
Our brothers from France, lucky in Mining,
were so delighted they raised a French flag
over their finds.   The Americans, not quite
as lucky, or happy, staggered up the hill
and ran the hapless men from their claims.
They later contended it was irresponsible
for the French Miners to raise their flag,
as it befouled the American Government.
Some have said it was more likely an easy
way to line their pockets.   So much for
Miner's justice!

   Whatever it was, and is, Mokelumne Hill
remains delightful.   And full of ghosts.
Here are the stories of two of them.

THE HOTEL LEGER
Wine, Women and Whoopie!

   Imagine ghostly parties that go on way
into the night.   Transparent bizarre
apparitions that loiter shamelessly in
doorways.   Floating figures that wind their
way thru the hallways and down corridors,
laughing and making merry.   You might as
well join the party.   They are not going
anywhere. Welcome to the Hotel Leger!

   In 1851 a newcomer to the hamlet, George
Leger, from Hesse Castle Germany, blew into
town.   An entrepreneur with cash in his
pocket and a love of good times, he was
immediately singled out as different from
the often crass and always dirty miners.
Thru some dealings in the community, shady
and sane, he soon found himself tripling his

investments, and with enough cash to build a one-story hotel. True to his heritage, he named it the Hotel de L'Europe (The European Hotel.) Soon he added a second story to be used for room and board, and converted the first floor into a general store. Never satisfied, he added a lavish dance floor for his parties. The Hotel soon became an elegant place to entertain in this part of the country, as many of the elite and famous from the world of arts and government made their way through his oak carved doors. George was happy here, and partied as only he knew how. An eye for the women, the beautiful and rich were his favorite. The best in alcohol and food was always on hand. He was in his element.

Unfortunately, in 1879 a portion of his hotel went up in flames. Undaunted, he rebuilt and renamed the place for good luck. "The new and better establishment shall be called the Hotel Leger" he told his friends. He fashioned himself a pillar of society!

Women, women, women! He loved them all. Being married never seemed to interfere. His bride died two years after the nuptials, probably a lucky break for her. Certainly vowing his everlasting love for his much younger wife at her funeral, (She was 25, he 43) he continued his lifestyle as he had before and during her time with him. Women, women, women.

But were the ladies that interested in him? Of couse! Why not? He was a dashing figure of a man, six foot tall, dark hair and moustache, in his sexual prime, and wealthy. One of the women he pursued noted he had "piercing eyes that beckoned for adventure."

Poor ole' George had the time of his life until he managed to fool with the wrong gal. W.H. Adams, Leger's friend and the owner of the stage company that had the Wells Fargo contract between Stockton and Sacramento, had a violent temper. His eyes set on a beautiful cultured young damsel he had been dating for quite some time, was tortured to hear she had been with Leger for the most part during his absences. He also owed Leger money, and under the circumstances thought better of repaying his debt. Over several bottles of whiskey he made a fateful decision. He hired a hit man to regain his girl. A few months later, the lone gunman hired for the job climbed the stairs to the living quarters of the Hotel Leger. He knocked on Room 7 and as the door opened he shot Leger. Point blank! The man fell mortally wounded into the arms of Adam's paramour. The blamable walked calmly down the stairs, passing those going up the other side to aid Leger. He crossed the street and was never seen again. A fitting augury to the story, it is believed Adam's lass took off with someone else anyway. Whether he had to repay the loan to Leger's creditors or family is not known. But he was the first up the stairs that fateful day on Leger's behalf, and as his friend was laid to rest, he led the crowd in tearful lament for his lost buddy. As a befitting omen, if you visit the pioneer cemetery today you will see that Adams was interred next to his ex-best friend making one wonder if now all is forgiven, as they continue to party together in the hereafter. Speculation aside, soon after Leger's death his spirit began showing up at the Hotel. Still over-seeing things, his friends in life started to feel uneasy, most especially Adams, for the secret was his alone. No one except he was aware of his involvement in Leger's demise until he fessed up years later. Maybe on his own deathbed. Never mind. Once they made the transition to the other side there was no animosity among

drinking buds. Many of the old crowd are
seen partying these days with Leger, Adam's
included.

Our dear friend Ron Miller, along with
his wife Joyce, purchased the Hotel in June
of 1987. He moved his kids into several
upstairs rooms. His pretty wife, a
schoolteacher, would join them later as
school let out. Several days later the
children came screaming from their bedroom.
"Someone told us to be quiet" they told
their Dad. Upon investigating he could find
no one. Later that day they went to Room
7, which had been George Leger's bedroom,
and where he died. The kids came running
to their father. "The man in that picture"
they told him, pointing to an old tin-type
on the wall. That was the man who told us
to be quiet." Ron shuddered. The photo
was of George Leger. Ron, always one to
wear a cowboy hat, remarked he often saw two
cowboy hats coming up the stairs in the
shadows on the wall. One was his......

Over the years during Leger's stint at
proprietor of the Hotel it served as
brothel, saloon, dance hall, country store,
and boarding house. During the renovations
of the building and through several new
owners since that time, the entities that
inhabit the structure, including Leger, take
most offence to the changes being made.
Tricks being played and many annoying spirit
games cause delays in the projects as only
the lifeless can do. "Most spirits do not
like change" the owners have told us. This
is universally true according to our
research. They prefer the familiarity of
the way things were as they knew them.
"Often our guests will complain about a man
chasing women down the halls late at night"
the proprietors told the authors. We tell
them, "It's just George in a rambunctious
mood." Things being moved around in the

building are commonplace, and George and his friends have no mercy on the cooking staff. "He moves things around the kitchen and drops things all over in the dining area. You never know when things are going to be missing. It's crazy!" an employee told us.

In February of 1997 we visited the Hotel Leger to become acquainted with the new owners, Mark and Nancy Jennings. Upon arriving I spoke to Mark about our investigation of his Hotel. He took my arm and guided me to the downstairs living room just behind the bar. "Then tell me" he asked, "Why can't we keep candles in the candelabrum?" He shook his head, "They are always all over the room."

I immediately called Rosie into the room. "I can see a lot of activity here" she told us. She got that impish look in her eyes. "There is a lot of sexual activity that goes on in this room. WOW! The parties!" She looked around, squinting her eyes so as not to miss anything. "As for the candelabrum" she said. "They are being thrown around by a bunch of drunken fools, having a good time. Sometimes they are just bumped over. People sure had a good time here."

They still are!

"The other night we had a very frightening experience" Nancy Jennings was to tell us. "For insurance purposes we were asked to put a surveillance camera up in the downstairs bar area. It is hooked up to our bedroom where we can see what is going on after hours. About three A.M. when the bar was closed and on one was left in the building except my husband and myself, I looked up to see smoke in the surveillance camera. I immediately alerted Mark. 'I think we have a fire down there' I told him." She shook her shoulders. "He immediately went down to investigate and there was no smoke or smell of anything burning. We sat there and watched the smoke on the camera until it slowly disappeared. Nothing explains what it is?" Our experts were able to identify the smoke like substance immediately. "It's a filmy substance called ectoplasm" they were able to confirm. Another guest was to see a face not her own in a mirror in Room 4. "The woman was prettier than I am" she said. "Besides frightening me, that was an annoying revelation."

Of all the places we researched and investigated for <u>Gold</u> <u>Rush</u> <u>Ghosts</u> the Hotel Leger is one of the most fascinating, and fun to visit. We suggest you stop by and see for yourself.

The Hotel Leger, where the spirit of George Leger and his friends continue to party.

NOTE: The Hotel Leger is located at:
        8304 Main Street
        Mokelumne Hill, CA. 95245
        (209) 286-1401
        Fax (209) 286-2105
They boast a room thirteen, a sun warmed pool, full bar, and elegant restaurant.

THE "STREET WALKER" GHOST OF MOKELUME HILL
A Window Peeper From The Past

Unlike the picture painted by the title of this story, the street walker ghost of Mokelumne Hill is not a woman of the oldest profession. Although, in actuality, that would be interesting wouldn't it? This street walking ghost is, in actuality, a man in his later years, one with a long black leather type coat, and a long salt and pepper beard. He likes to hang around the old buildings on Main Street, and can often be seen in the fields at the end of the road. He mostly shows up late at night, although at times, the early morning hours in the mist and dew, he can be found staring at the street. He seems rather lost, or just meandering. He is certainly not in a hurry so nothing is pressing with him as far as we are concerned, and he rather likes to startle the residents before he smiles and slowly disappears. Who he is no one knows. Who he could be, history does not offer possible explanations. But he has been here many years, and walks a wide path through the town.

In 1992 a woman from the town told the authors that she saw him quite frequently when hanging her laundry on the line in her back yard. A country setting with a lawn that backs up to an uncultivated hill, he liked to stand behind her and watch her work. Undaunted after years of his being there, she takes him for granted. "He has never appeared inside the house, either now or before my husband died. As long as he just likes the yard, he can stay. It's not like he is always around, just on occasion. I can live with it."

It is also noted that the walker likes

the old pioneer part of the cemetery, where
he walks among the grave markers. He can be
seen looking into the windows of the shops
of the town, most often the older ones on
Main Street.   He just puts his nose up to
the panes and peers in.   No one seems to
want him to leave the community, and he does
not seem to be in distress, so our psychics
did not try to contact him or ask him if he
wanted to be released to another dimension.

Walk on, our friend, and relish in your
life of a simpler time among the things you
enjoyed.   We hope you're happy.

12.

NEVADA CITY
Mighty Ghosts and More

The year was 1850, and folks flocked to a meeting in what would become Nevada City. It seemed men were pulling pounds of gold, sometimes daily, from nearby Deer Creek. The winters were harsh, cruel in fact, as frostbite and pneumonia took their toll. The hardy, with gold in their hearts, were determined to bare the hardships to find their fortunes. The community had grown to over a thousand residents and it seemed proper a name should be found for the town that was growing up around them. After many names were thrown into the pot, Nevada was decided on, a Spanish word meaning "snow-covered". The name pretty much pleased everyone, and the menfolk kissed their loved ones good-bye as they again picked up pan and shovel to hopefully make their dreams come true, quick fortunes in gold. All was well.

Fourteen years later another meeting was to be held. It was found the town of Nevada had no claim on it's hurriedly picked name. It was accused by the state of Nevada of having "stolen" this name. If you cannot join them.....the undaunted residents said disgusted. Nevada added a "City" to the end of their community's name so as not to be confused with the state of Nevada. The residents shrugged their shoulders, laughed, and resumed the business of the day, the search for gold.

The 1850's and 1860's were prosperous for Nevada City. Despite seven fires the town grew and the hardy remained. Fires! They are surely synonymous with the Gold Rush days. Yet, they continued to build. The folks of Nevada City being no fools, they finally decided to form a volunteer fire department against destruction. Fate again took it's place among what is known as the mighty fires of the mother lode. This time it leveled most of the town. This time the town was rebuilt, primarily in brick. But they got smarter still in 1861, when it was decided there should be two firehouses, to safehouse their investments. They were unimaginatively named Firehouse No.1, and Firehouse No.2.

According to a representative of the Searles Historical Library in Nevada City, "The residents of the town could not decide where to build the firehouse. The Main Street merchants wanted the firehouse down there, and the Broad Street merchants wanted to have it up there. They could never agree, and so they divided and each built their own. The wives of the Broad Street merchants went door to door and collected the needed funds faster than the Main Street merchants, so though it was called Firehouse No. 2, the Broad Street Firehouse was constructed first, by about nine months." They were, and are to this day, as different in size and structure as could be possible. Firehouse No. 1 gave citizens reason to boast, as it was the finest, best equipped, and most beautiful of its day, a wooden and brick two-story structure, with Victorian bell tower and gingerbread trim added around the year 1866. Both served their purpose with updates until the year 1938, when a new, modern firehouse was constructed on

Broad Street, a short distance from the former. When last checked, Firehouse No. 2 was a warehouse. Firehouse No.1 houses the Nevada City Historical Museum, and all the elusive ghosts therein. So began our search for the incredible legends, unfathomable specters, and chilling ectoplasmatic encounters in Nevada City.

NEVADA CITY HISTORICAL MUSEUM
Red-heads, Ruckus, and Rebellious Phantoms

We do not know if it was haunted during it's firehouse days, but strange things certainly started to happen by the time firehouse was turned into a museum and the Gold Rush mementoes began to arrive.

Hjalmer E.Berg, a former director of the museum, was to notice "Cold areas and drafts in the building that were unaccountable."
He repeated hearing footsteps when no one was around. "I was alone, yet not alone," he was to say. The man told of a Jesuit Priest and two affiliates who toured the museum. When they reached the second floor, they turned to ask him who the red-haired woman in old-fashioned clothing was who sat down to play the antique piano the museum had inherited from an old whorehouse. As delicately and cautiously as he possible could, he explained the truth. "She is one of our ghosts," he said. He was quick to add that no such red-haired person had ever been employed at the museum. It was assumed the redhead liked the piano when she was employed at the house of questionable repute, and decided to stay with it here at its new residence. A former president of the Historical Society once carefully shut a cabinet door, only to have it fly back open

at her. When this repeated several times, for no apparent reason, and being aware of the many ghosts of the Nevada County Historical Museum, she told the unseen presence to "Stop this at once!" The cabinet door remained shut, but there were loud and unquestionable footsteps walking away behind her. She knew she was alone in the building. At least there were no other "living" people in the place!

Guests experience ghosts upstairs at the old piano, at the hutch, and the rocking chair. She apparently is the same brazen redhead, just doin' her thing. Sometimes she sings, sometimes she struts, and sometimes she sits and rocks.

There are reports on file of another spirit woman upstairs at the Firehouse Museum, this one in Victorian attire. She is rummaging through a cabinet, the doors of which are padlocked.

Ghost news sells copy. Soon the media flocked to the museum. On Wednesday, February 13,1974, the Sacramento Bee front page headline read: "That Nudge in the Ribs in Nevada City House is Pushed Around by Exorcising S.F.Visitor." It tells of first-hand ghost sightings, of the feeling of being "pushed and shoved" while in the building and a plea from this former director for a psychic to come to the building and exorcise the ghosts.

"It was the oriental ghosts that frightened me, stated Cheryl Johnson and her new husband Carl, speaking of their visit to the museum in 1987. A thousand-year-old Taoist shrine from a joss (God) house in Grass Valley had found it's way here. Believed to be the oldest in North America, guests to the museum complain of feeling pushed and tripped when they stand before the shrine. "As I stood before the shrine, several figures of Chinese men materialized

before me, Johnson stated.   "There were
several of them, some kneeling, one walking
around slowly, his head bent.   I blinked a
few times and they faded away.   I heard a
low, moaning sound, and my son heard what he
described as chanting.   We turned to leave,
and my son fell over as if something had
shoved him."

The piece in the museum you must not miss
is the 1880 photograph of an Irish miner by
the name of Carrigan.   The portrait is of an
ageing man with white hair and beard.   To
the side   of   Carrigan,   in   the   same
photograph, is the image of a young boy.
When the film was developed Carrigan and the
photographer could find no reason for this.
Who was this little boy in the photograph?
Carrigan had   been   thinking   about   his
childhood when the photo was taken and he
offered perhaps the image was of himself as
a child. But he did not know for sure.
Stranger still, the longer you look into the
photograph, the more spirit faces appear.

The amazing Nevada County Historical
Museum is open April 1 thru October 31, from
11:00 AM to 4:00 PM. Visiting this historic
firehouse will give you more than your
money's worth.

THE RED CASTLE INN
And The Ghosts 'Live' There Too

If you haven't already become acquainted
with the beautiful Red Castle Inn on one of
the numerous television shows that have done
stories on it's captivating history and it's
ghosts, we are presenting an in depth view.
You will be charmed by the host, the
hostess, and the loveliness that is all
around you, which in its perfection, brings

us back to a different time. And among the
amazing thing you may find are ghosts that
act like they own the place. Indeed, at one
time, some of them did! They have resided
here, you see, in all their glory, through a
succession of owners, remodelings, and
occupants. They are, in a word, content,
and seem determined to stay through time
immortal.

The most visible of these apparitions
seem to be the original owner and builder of
the mansion, his devoted wife Abigail, and
the "Lady in Gray," his children's
dependable governess who continues to serve.

The beautiful red brick building was
completed in 1860, a four story masterpiece
at the direction of John Williams. A former
merchandiser from Illinois, it fulfilled a
lifelong promise made to his wife Abigail.
With elaborate gingerbread trim the final
addition, he sat back and admired his work.
His faithful wife had waited many years for
this house, and he knew she would now feel
finally at home. Abigail knew of the
fineries of life, and managed to furnish the
mansion in such splendor John Williams was
amazed. She had married him at the tender
age of 15, a girl really, and Williams was
about to give her back the life she was
formerly accustomed to.

From the day they met, they had eyes only
for each other. The only disappointment of
their marriage was Abigail's inability to
produce a large family. (In those days it
was always considered the woman's fault for
lack of conception). She did however,
produce him two children, a girl who died an
infant, and a son they named Loring Wallace.
Next to her husband, Abigail loved children,
and any child with a sad tale went straight
to her heart and into her home. Later in
life she was to take on a succession of
foster children to raise and love.

But in the early years, there was no time for thoughts like these! Life was hard. Years passed, as John had his hands in venture after venture in his search for a worryless lifestyle. When nothing really 'panned' out (pun intended) he decided to follow Abigail's brother to the Mother Lode. People were making fortunes there, right? Why not get his share! Word had spread of the riches being found around Sutter's Mill. John, the adventurer, Abigail, and their 17 year old son Loring set out for Coloma, the land of promise.

It soon became apparent the hardships of the mining camps was too much for Abigail. A decision was made to send her to live at her brother's home in Napa Valley. Thus accomplished, Father and son toiled the mud and muck of the American River.

Not being especially successful, the men then moved toward the foothills. In 1850 they settled at Deer Creek Dry Diggins, which is now known as Nevada City. Missing his wife unbearably, John doodled a sketch of the home he hoped to build for her. In his letter he described in detail the type of land he had discovered, and promised to buy as soon as their fortune came in. Years had passed, and age was against him. He was now fifty-five, the work load almost unbearable. It was this dream house, and his promise to his lovely Abigail which kept his aging body and emotional state together. He continued to toil the land, day after day, year after year. He could not fail. It was his last chance to fulfill that promise.

The Williams men faced many hardships as did most of the men in the gold fields, but eventually, in 1860 John acquired enough gold to buy that plot of land he promised his wife. He would now build her their dream house. Fate being everything, the land he loved and purchased was called Prospect Hill. Those days behind him, the word prospector held no bad memories. He was through with the mud and muck the fields and streams. He would not look back.

Loring Wallace and his father eagerly began construction of their mansion. It would have four floors not including the brick framing and wrap-around veranda. Approximately 4,000 sq. feet, plans were made to include sixteen rooms and a utility basement. For Abigial, his bride of aristocratic birth, he would provide two formal parlors for her parties and other important occasions. He knew she loved to entertain. This house would have two master bedrooms, one for Abigail and John, the other for Loring Wallace and his new bride. They continued to build, a kitchen, entry, and other bedrooms were painstakingly and precisely added. It.'s a good thing they did. Over the years, up to 11 children and foster children would make their home at the Red Castle. Of these children (many orphaned by the hardships of the times), had their choice of bedrooms on the third or fourth floor. The Wallace's hired a complete staff to oversee the mansion. The governess for the children soon moved in and secured a bedroom on the fourth floor to always be near her charges. For all eternity she is known only as the "Lady in Gray", but played an enormous roll in the Wallace's lives, both back then, and since their death.

Both couples moved into their dream home. Loring Wallace's new wife, Cornelia Elizabeth Humes, was a woman of social standing and fit well into the family. The son was an ambitious man, with dreams of magnitude. With more energy than most men his age, and brains to match, he could not loose. Taking Cornelia as his wife proved to be an asset to his career, as well as his

164

personal life. In rapid succession they produced four sons, during which time he obtained a degree in Law, and served as under-sheriff of Nevada City. He started a successful law practice in 1864, and was appointed district attorney soon after that.

Ten wonderful years past swiftly, as John and Abigail enjoyed their mansion, their son and daughter-in-law, grandchildren, foster children, and friends within the community. Respected members of society, they loved the luxury of entertaining lavishly in their beautiful home. Abigail and Cornelia were to oversee many community events, including weddings for the elite, and other festive occasions held around their perfectly manicured terraced gardens. As if the family could do no wrong, John was elected Justice of the Peace, and was now called "Squire" by the townspeople. Things could not be better for the Williams family......

Unfortunate but true, all things come to an end. Thus we are reminded of the saying 'enjoy today for tomorrow...'

Squire John Williams died on Wednesday February 8, 1871 at the age of 68. He died in the arms of his beloved Abigail. Never considered the affectionate type, she wept uncontrollably as they took his lifeless body from her arms. The man she had loved her whole life was gone. After all their struggles to secure the lifestyle they had dreamed of, the unfairness of only having had a few years together was unbearable. John had suffered immensely at the end, probably of cancer, and Abigail never left his side during his last brave fight. She insisted his funeral have all the pomp and circumstance befitting such a great man, and his body was laid out (as was the custom of the day), in one of the ornate living rooms he had built for her. Friends and neighbors, the elite, dignitaries, came to pay their respects and try to offer condolences to the inconsolable Abigail. So many years married, so few years together, as he tried to fulfill his promise. In retrospect, she would have rather lived in a shack than loose her husband.

After John's elaborate funeral service at the house, people bundled up and huddled together as they joined the long procession of wagons following the coffin through the snow and sleet, the bitter cold, to see him forever laid to rest in the old cemetery.

Or at least his earthly body forever laid to rest. Our guess is he didn't even attend his own funeral. John's 'spirit', being smarter than most, stayed home in the warm Red Castle.

Of course things had to go on. After the funeral, John Wallace took over the finances as his father had done before him. Most of their holdings were in businesses and property rentals. His family as well as many others had fallen victim to the ravaging fires of the time. They had to rebuild their empire more than once, and this cost money. Loring Wallace could clearly see their fortune dwindling.

The son inherited these problems upon his father's death, but being an acute businessman, worked hard to increase the family's holdings. Nothing much changed on the home front however, except there was now that unescapable sorrow in his mother's eyes. During this grieving period, the "Lady in Gray" took over the care of the children. She had been with the family for many years, and knew exactly what Abigail and Cornelia wanted for their children. The governess was dowdy of dress, small in stature, but dearly loved by the children, and was, indeed, a very kind and honorable woman. Her name and background are lost to us. History will never reveal why she never married or had children of her own. Perhaps her lover died in the gold field, or she had some other tragedy that made her wish to give her life completely to anothers family in disregard to her own. But this is speculation. We do know she took her job seriously, chastising the indiscretions and catering to the whims of the younger residents at the Red Castle. She had a special way of dealing with each circumstance, and administering her own brand of appropriate action. She was given a free hand with which to raise the children. She loved them, and a little terrier dog which she often carried under her arm.

Three years later, learning to deal with her grief, and just as a smile was appearing on Abigail's face, her son Loring Wallace died.

Again on a dismal February day, this woman thought her heart would break. As his father before him, John Wallace passed through this life and into the next in his wife's arms, in his bedroom, in the beautiful mansion. Knowing the end was near, he sold his worldly goods to Cornelia for $1,000, with the exclusion of the home which was to remain his mothers. Eerily, as they had done all things together in life, Loring Wallace's funeral was then held at the Red Castle, at precisely the same time and day of the week as his father's.

The men were gone now, and neither women knew the slightest about the financial empire their husbands owned and took care of. Without proper ability to oversee the operations, they feared edging toward bankruptcy. One by one, as money depleted, they relieved their servants of their duties. At the end only the governess remained, our 'lady in gray.' Without care, the grounds went to weed and disrepair. The house a shambles. Pain and disaster!

Frail since birth, Cornelia Elizabeth died suddenly the morning of June 18, 1883. Abigail was left to continue by herself. These were her declining years. In 1891, feeble and old, Abigail suffered her final indignity. It came when the once robust woman realized she could no longer pick up a rake to remove the leaves and pine needles from the roof. Admitting to her fate, she sold her dream home with gardens and adjoining lots for $1,500 in gold coin. Abigail gave up her earthly life in Southern California, where it is reported she lived with one of her many foster children. She welcomed death, for only then could she come back to her beloved Red Castle. Rumor has it the "Lady in Gray" never did exit the Red Castle. With the knowledge that Abigail had sold and would soon be leaving the stately mansion, she was found in her bedroom, dead in her sleep.

Exquisite, it holds a family's secrets, and we understand why they insist on staying around.

Of course the mansion was not known as the Red Castle in those days, and we know because so many years have passed that truths fall into "maybe" and "perhaps." But from here our story moves into other dimensions of reality, as the parties who witnessed the events are very much alive, and have given their testimonies as only they experienced them.

One such person is Jim Schaar, who purchased the run-down mansion in 1963, along with all the unnatural phenomena which is commonplace within the grounds and household.

"I grew up on the Monterey Peninsula amid all the beautiful old buildings and homes," Schaar said, "and I always had a dream of owning and restoring one. Seeing the Red Castle was the closest I have ever come to having a metaphysical experience. The moment I saw it, I knew I had to have it. I signed on the dotted line just hours after first laying eyes on it. Looking back, it seemed as if someone or something had taken hold of me. Later, when I returned home, I had a case of buyer's remorse. I truly had no idea how I would pay for it, but I just could not pick up the phone to cancel the deal."

Schaar's association with the Red Castle turned into a profitable one, as well as a learning experience of the nervous kind.

"I hired a handyman soon after moving in, and we went to work restoring the building. We started laughing about always looking over our shoulders, because we both had the unearthly feeling someone was watching us. When we looked around, there was no one there." Then, late one afternoon, the workman shed some light on the mystery. The specter materialized in front of him, showing concern about the work we were doing. He was able to describe the ghost in vivid detail, as the image remained fixed for some time. He later described it as "an old man ghost, in the attire of the 1800's....a black frock coat like a judge would wear....an old man doing a routine inspection, seeing how the work was coming along."

"I really didn't want to believe in ghosts," Schaar was to tell us. "I was afraid I might meet one face to face."

Jerry Ames owned the mansion from 1978 to 1986, and although he never saw a ghost through the years, he managed to keep his living guests and spirit residents happy if not, in all cases, segregated!

"Strange little things were always happening that we couldn't quite put our finger on," he was to explain. "For instance, my partner told me the Red Castle 'hid things.' He mentioned putting things somewhere and then could not find them. Later they would be found in another spot or part of the house.

"I think one of the strangest occurrences happened after a snow storm. There was a foot and a half of snow on the ground when a guest asked,'Who is the man on the deck? He's dressed rather strangely, in black and with a tall hat.' I knew of no guest that fit that description, and so we went to investigate. There was no one on the deck, and we were both startled to find no footprints leading to the deck. No mortal man could have been out there.

"Another time a guest asked me who was the oddly-dressed man crossing from one room to another room which was locked. At the time I knew the rooms were empty as the occupants had left to dine in town. The guest swore he had seen a sober-faced person in a hooded robe."

One of the finest examples of materialization was to happen to an unsuspecting studious, middle-aged, male guest.

"The poor gentleman came into the doorway of the parlor," said Ames. "He was ashen. 'Who is David?' he asked, obviously shaken.

"We did not know what he was talking about. We checked our register and we had no one in the Inn by that name. As his story unfolded, we got our first glimpse of the children's governess, the Lady in Gray."

"I was asleep in bed when I was awaken by a pressure on my legs," the gentleman said. "As I got my bearing, I realized I couldn't move them because someone or something I could not see was sitting on them. As I struggled to push whatever it was off of me, out of the corner of my eye I saw a young woman standing in the room. She was dressed in gray, and seemed angry, 'David, DAVID!' she said, as if to reprimand a disobedient child. The pressure on my legs lifted immediately, as if someone had gotten up, and she swiftly faded away."

During the years Jim Schaar owned the Inn, a very unusual experience was reported. "I had a New Year's Eve Victorian dress party," Schaar told us. "It was held for guests and townsfolk, and lasted well into the wee hours. Everyone was having a great time."

One woman, however, a non-drinker, had enough of the merry making and about midnight retired for the evening. As she settled into bed a woman came in, dressed for the occasion and carrying a small dog. She was dressed in a Victorian gown, and the guest remembering it being a soft gray color. She thought it odd her visitor should have a dog, for surely she had not seen one at the party.

The 'Lady in Gray' sat at the foot of the bed and patting the small dog made pleasant conversation, talking about the party and other things of interest in a casual way to two people who had just met. After a while the woman stood and shifted the dog to her other arm. She smiled and said "Everything is going to be fine!" With that she left and closed the door.

The tired guest was a little puzzled about the last comment, but being so tired gave it little thought before falling asleep.

The next morning the guest looked for her new friend at breakfast. When she didn't see her, she inquired. The woman was told that all the guests who had been at the party were present. Besides which, no dog was or had been on the premises, to anyone's knowledge. She never saw her visiting friend again, but she had perfectly described the 'Lady in Gray.'

We could not possibly list all the sightings of the 'Lady in Gray,' nor the sightings of old John Williams. The 'Gray Lady' has been seen in the Gold Room and hallways, also in the bedrooms, and most of all, on the top floor where she and the children resided.

The current owners, the delightful Conley and Mary Louise Weaver, are certainly not exempt. They have had their experiences with ghostly phenomena. Mary Louise tells of a couple who went upstairs to the 'Gray Lady's' bedroom to retire for the evening. A strange light appeared. There was not a light on in the mansion, and it was not a full moon. In fact, it was a very dark night. There seemed no mortal reason for the light to be in the room. They felt an uneasy stillness as the unexplained illumination circled around the foot of the bed.

After blinking their eyes several times, and holding their breath, the light disappeared. Other less adventurous people might have wanted another room, but they stayed through the night.

During the same evening, Mary Louise was having her own light problems. She tells of going to a restroom which used to be a toy room off the children's bedroom, and finding the light on. She thought it strange as no one was around and the guests had retired for the evening. She checked her watch. It was about midnight. Shrugging her shoulders, she turned the light off.

The next morning while making her rounds, she noticed the light was back on. This time the door was closed. The room is directly below the bedroom where the guests experienced their mysterious light.

Employees of Conley and Mary Louise have had their moments with the ghosts of the Red Castle. One told of having a glimpse of a ghost in Civil War uniform with brass buttons in one of the children's bedrooms. A housekeeper, cleaning one of the bathrooms, looked into the hall to clearly see the' Lady in Gray' drift by.

A few years ago the owners were startled to discover the balcony on the third floor locked. Under normal circumstances this would not be unusual, except this time it was locked from the outside. There are no stairs, no trellis, no way to exit the balcony from the outside.

Letters from former guests are forever being sent to the Weavers. One from a Doctor reads in part "I had the pleasure of staying at the Red Castle the evening of December 8th.

"I had an experience I wanted to share with you. (I noted in the Visitors Diary a couple of other people had experiences too).

"Around 10 pm I turned out the light and got in bed. I felt a pressure like my back was being pushed on/someone was sitting on me. It lasted about 30 seconds.The room was very cold for that time and smelled sort of 'woodsy.' I was scared at first but then the pressure felt kind of nurturing. I turned the light back on as soon as it stopped but there was nothing there. I didn't hear anything either.

Any information you could share with me would be deeply appreciated. I do plan to come and stay again........"

Another person wrote: "The rooms on the third floor are occupied by Laura Jean. Her presence is very strong." This same person later wrote, "The next thing occurred as I first dozed off: I was being kissed the most tender, sweet, goodnight kiss by her. She relates with the Inn's guests that we are her children that she cares for." And then, "I did fall asleep and awoke after another experience: Children jumping into bed, then they were kittens being put to bed by her and the children."

And then another letter (In part)," This is our 3rd Anniversary which we chose to spend at the Red Castle Inn.

I was kept awake all night and experienced a woman speaking to me. To visualize, I would say she was over the bed, leaning slightly forward and speaking to me. She was wearing a dark cape and what looked like a dark matching cap. I remember being very comfortable and feeling pleased as this woman had to have been one of the most kind and loving individuals ever to have walked this earth. It was uplifting and fulfilling to experience her presence."

Conley and Mary Louise are often the victims of ghostly pranks, or misunderstandings. "Remember the other day?" Conley was to say to his wife during our visit. He turned to address this author. "I was in one of the bedrooms on the second floor and saw what I thought was Mary Louise walk into another bedroom. The person

174

had on one of those long skirts Mary Louise so often wears so I assumed it was her. I called out to her but she did not answer. Then I saw Mary Louise coming up the stairs. I went into the bedroom I thought I saw Mary Louise go into, but it was empty."

Ah, the ghosts 'live' on!

It's lovely, it's enjoyable, it's enchanting to visit with the Weavers. Mary Louise is the perfect hostess, a combination of experience, charm and warm hospitality. Conley has one of those great dry sense of humors that is so infectious. Over the years they have made it a project to completely bring the Red Castle back to it's original style and furnishings. I am certain they would be happy to tell you about the ghosts if you ask them, but then again, you just might see them for yourself.

We know there are ghosts at the Red Castle Inn. There are children, the "Gray Lady" and kittens. There is Laura Jean and a Terrier dog. There are probably a host of others we have not gotten to know as yet. But the most heartwarming to grace the mansion are the spirits of Abigail and John. Guests have reported seeing them walking, hand in hand, in the garden.

NOTE: The Red Castle Inn is located at:
      109 Prospect St
      Nevada City, CA.95959
      530-265-5135
A bed and Breakfast, they provide a lovely breakfast for their guests.

13.

GRASS VALLEY
Gold, George, Ghosts, and Lola

It was 1850 when a man by the name of George Knight stepped on a piece of quartz. Placing it in his hand, he was amazed to see gold flakes interlaced throughout the rock. The rumors flew faster than he could put the sparkle in his pocket. Grass Valley had just assured it's spot on the map!

As word of his find was being circulated, new and better techniques for mining were being developed. Progress being made, Grass Valley was to find itself one of the richest gold-producing towns in California. It's most famous mine, The Empire, produced in upward to 6 million ounces of gold while in operation.

Before George's find, Grass Valley could be considered nothing more than a insignificant mining camp. This towns fire history wiped out over 300 buildings, stopping just short of leveling the whole community. As always, that old Gold Rush comradeship kicked in. Rebuilding was the call for those days.

One of the most notorious and colorful of Gold Rush characters not only lived in Grass Valley, but had her house saved from that fire. Born Eliza Gilbert in Ireland, the beautiful Lola Montez had a past to challenge her talent. She was the high topic at every camp, "have you seen her" did you know she", "have you heard that....." To add to her mystique, she could often be seen around the camps with one or more of her wild pets, a wolf, grizzly cubs..........

But enough of that. It is another book. For now I have something even more important to tell you about Grass Valley. Things that link the past to the present. I hope you will visit the old Hardscrabble Building, on your way to having lunch or dinner at the Holbrooke Hotel. You might have unseen guests at your table. Then again, you could make some lonely ghosts happy.

THE HARDSCRABBLE BUILDING
The Coffin Maker's Remains?

Does he walk the streets of Grass Valley? Perhaps visit his favorite table at the Holbrooke Hotel? Or does he spend his days in the back room of the Hardscrabble Building perfecting his craft? Does the 1800's undertaker the renown author Vincent Gaddis refers to in Gold Rush Ghosts #1, the one with a hankerin' for making coffins, seem destined to be forever associated with the Hardscrabble Building at 107 West Main Street in Grass Valley? Did he love his work that much, or perhaps by preparing so many of his friends to go on before him, he is now content to remain where he last enjoyed their company. Ah, his funeral parlor! And maybe, just maybe, most of them are still with him!

Records differ on the year the old Hardscrabble Building was constructed. Whether 1852 or 1856, we know the building was designed to the exact specifications of our friendly undertaker. A room for preparation, a room for viewing, and a room for building the final vessels. Perfect for his needs.

But after about twenty-five corpses passed through it's doors, pale and cold yet beautifully made-up, rumor has it strange visions began to occur. At night a film, a gathered fog, could be seen floating toward the door and then entering the building. Later that night it could be seen exiting.

Placing one of his newly finished coffin products in the window to show it off, the undertaker would be confused as someone from the street would come in and inquire who the "stiff" in the wood box was. The undertaker would have to explain the casket was empty. He would put his arm around the person and then show them himself. Yup! No occupants. "If you want to see someone dead I have someone in the back room" he probably told them. There were few takers. But what about today? The building of late has been occupied by a number of businesses. We remember two of them we enjoyed visiting, the Hardscrabble Antique Emporium, and the Hardscrabble Coin Store. Neither of those businesses remain in the building. For so many years these stories have abound concerning the incarnate spirits that inhabit the place. We wonder if some of the fleeting visitors from the mortuary days had stayed on to "greet their friends as the time came?"

We must find out if the current occupants are aware of any transparent, bizarre, or glassy figures entertaining them on rainy dismal days inside the building, or if everything is now still. If nothing else, it will be great fun speculating as you pass by, or go in to shop.

THE HOLBROOKE HOTEL
The Tale of Table 15
And The Doodling Desk Clerk

There is definitely a favorite table in the restaurant of the Holbrooke Hotel. Table 15. And it appears to be the preference of both paying customers, and those who don't build up a tab. Folks in the living experience, and those from the past. Or, at least, those who's living experience was played out in another time.

Built in 1851, the Holbrooke is now a California Registered Historical Landmark. (# 914.) Always a colorful and popular place, in it's heyday the building saw the likes of Presidents Ulysses S.Grant, James A. Garfield, and Benjamin Harrison walk through it's doors. Lush and extravagant, the Holbrooke was host to many of the most talented and entertaining people of the day, such as Mark Twain, Bret Harte, dancer Lotta Crabtree, and the infamous actress/ dancer Lola Montez. The Holbrooke Hotel boasts it's present bar has been in continuous operation since 1852. Thats a lot of drinks! At that time it was known as the Golden Gate Saloon, and believed to have served the needs of Black Bart well!

But we are here to confirm or deny reports that have come back to our office concerning the appearance of two spirit men who grace this business with their presence, and then are gone. One, a tall balding gentleman with a white band around his arm and pencil balanced behind one ear, seems to know the other, a man dressed in black, with a top hat. Both are often seen around Table 15. Our job is to separate the living from the past. We are not trying to forcibly remove the spirits from the building of cause. They appear to want to stay, and are no real problem to the management. Indeed their presence is calming and something that sets the Holbrooke apart from the other businesses in the area. Separate, then, is probably not the right word. Identify is closer. Identify which of the customers are spirits, how often they come here, what they want, and why they are here in the first place.

Stories have come to Gold Rush Ghosts about people who disappear in the dining area of the Holbrooke Hotel. Stories abound of talking folks who can not be seen, and strange smoke clouds in the bar, even though, at this time, smoking is illegal in the restaurants and lounges of California.

Our psychic was to visit the building three days prior to our interview with Peggy Levine, the very able and truthful manager of the Holbrooke. With Peggy there was no game playing to try and get the Hotel's name in print. She readily admitted to never having seen a ghost. She was forthright and honest, something we deeply respect, as she told Gold Rush Ghosts.

"I love old buildings" she told us. "I would never choose to live in a new building. I would never choose to take care of a new building. I just like old buildings."

She thought about her past. "You know, I have always lived in old buildings, in fact my house was built in 1867 and it's right up the street here. I grew up in a house that wasn't that old, it was built in the 20's, but I have lived in Victorians and places like that. Every place we travel we look for architecture and old buildings."

Then she explained her experiences within the Holbrooke "I had a professor once who was tied to feelings" she told Robert Reppert during their interview. "I don't have that. People, you know, you hear things, you feel things. You feel like people are here sometimes, especially when it is quiet. In the rooms upstairs, well, you know, you just feel like someone is there. I believe I like old buildings so much because there is a presence of people there."

Waitresses and other staff persons have certainly seen the ghosts. One talked of seeing a man in a hat sitting at table 15 as she went by. "He was reading a newspaper" she said, and she knew he must have just come in as he had not been waited on as yet. When she turned around to serve him, he was gone. Disappeared. "Just like that!" she said. There was no time for him to have gotten up and exited the building. Besides, he looked so content sitting there reading........

"It's funny about Table 15" other employees and friends of the restaurant were to share with us. "People gravitate to that side of the room. If Table 15 is occupied, the tables around it will be filled, and the rest of the restaurant empty. Funny too about Table 15, is the way couples always sit together on one side of the table, as if the other side is already occupied. There is just something about that side of the building."

Our psychics returned with the following report. "There is a natural vortex past the register desk, and to the left side of the building". (This was later to be confirmed to be in the same area as Table 15.) The vortex, with its extreme energy field, allows spirits to enter and exit the building with ease."

As an experiment, anyone with the desire to feel the vortex energy, need only stand to the front of the table, and close their eyes. It is then that they will feel their body is moving, perhaps swaying from side to side. Some people feel a dizziness, some feel they are going to fall down. This is especially true if entities are about, and trying to enter or exit. Because of it's existence, it should make this part of the room very interesting. Disembodied spirits usually feel cold if they pass through you, and a vortex can be extremely warm and inviting. I can certainly see why people would be drawn to that side of the restaurant" Robert told us.

Our psychic then spoke of some of the spirits that were found. "One man here, appeared to have worked in the building in the 1800's. He finds it amusing that when his time came he was replaced with another man who looked almost exactly like him. He is laughing about this 'cloning' thing that 'folks are making such a fuss about today'. He says the other guy is as 'close to a cloning that he has ever seen. (Hah!).' He works at the front desk, is a clerk, and talks of being very bored at times. "He plays with his pencil to keep occupied" our psychic related, "because the management would get upset if they caught him reading or anything. He was always to appear official."

"His friend visits from time to time. That would account for the man with the hat. He comes in quite often, sometimes after his business is closed for the night. Sometimes, if his friend is working the 'graveyard' shift, he will just stop by to visit and talk. They have become quite close having been together as friends for over 100 years."

Robert then picked up the vibrations of two women, both from the Gold Rush days. "Sarah Jean is here" he faxed to our office. "She is an entertainer, a singer. She stays upstairs when performing. She has with her a small child she calls little Harry, and she tells us her husband is Horace. He has been gone a long time, and she fears he might have lost his life searching for gold around Coloma."

A few days later, during their interview, Robert was to be amazed when Peggy brought out the ledger for the old Holbrooke Hotel. There, on the bottom of many pages, and throughout the book, day by day, were penciled in doodles. There were circles, box like drawings, and interesting designs.

The flag went up. Was the ghost our resident psychic saw that of the clerk? It would appear so. The man with the hat? Perhaps the undertaker from the building across the street. What he was able to communicate with the spirits and the description the waitress gave, it is all the same.

Thank you Peggy, for your hospitality, and your honesty has been rewarded. You manage a very haunted hotel, and the kindest compliment, the ghosts that respect your privacy.

NOTE:The Holbrooke Hotel, Restaurant and Saloon is located at:

> 212 W. Main Street
> Grass Valley,CA. 95945
> (530) 273-1353
> (800) 933-7077

The lovely Victorian style Holbrooke Hotel features antiques in all rooms, private sitting areas and balconies. All rooms have a private bath, some with claw-foot tubs, and for your enjoyment, a continental breakfast is served each morning in the library. Brunch,lunch or dinner is served in

the elegant dining room or courtyard. The
Holbrooke Hotel provides a lovely setting
for weddings, receptions, group meetings,
family reunions, and corporate retreats.
They are ready to help you make memorable,
all your special functions.

The undertaker and the clerk. Are these
friends still here?

14

DOWNIEVILLE
The Indelible Stain

Nestled in a basin walled by sheer, pine-covered mountainsides, Downieville lies at 3,000 feet across the upper Yuba River. The seat of Sierra County, it is a pleasant, picturesque community of less than a thousand residents. Once the population numbered in the thousands. The gallows, last used for its grim purposes in 1885, is still on display, probably to remind that retribution is still a threat against crime. As in much of the gold country, fire did it's best to destroy evidence of history.

In November of the bustling year of 1849, Major William Downie arrived at the site with a motley band of followers. The group consisted of an Irishman, and Indian, ten black ex-sailors, and a gentleman of somewhat mysterious ancestry named Jim Crow. Happily, he never knew that his name would be identified with racial discrimination years later in America's Southland.

The major had noticed that the higher one went in the northern gold country, the larger became the nuggets. So he and his cohorts began climbing, despite grim warnings that winter was closing in. He was a man of great determination which approached foolhardiness.

Upon arrival to the area, the men found

the river filmed with ice and a bitter wind blowing the snow into fleecy clouds.

Downie had his men cut down small trees with their hatchets and erect crude cabins.

Then he put them to work panning on the snow-covered river bars. It was cold, very cold, but they were encouraged by gravel rich with nuggets and yellow grains.

After only a few weeks, provisions began to run low, and decisions had to be made to avoid starvation. The major divided the recovered gold among nine of the miners and sent them to get food and supplies in the lower country. With one exception, all decided to continue looking for gold in a warmer climate and they vanished in the maelstrom of mining camps.

Only faithful Jim Crow came back in the spring, just in time to save Downie and three remaining miners from starvation. The major and his remaining companions quickly recovered, but now they had far too many competitors to share the wealth. Jim had been followed by a small army of gold-hungry prospectors who had heard the strikes were best in the Sierra foothills. Surrounding camps appeared on every bar and flat.

Downieville may well have been the richest region in the Gold Rush. At one camp the three owners filled their tin cups with gold dust every day. They named it Tin Cup Diggins. Once when Jim Crow had boiled a 14 pound salmon he found gold flakes on the bottom of the pot. In only eleven day's four men took $12,000 worth from a claim 60 feet square. On Durgan's Flat, where the Sierra County Courthouse now stands, $80,000 in gold was found in the first half of 1850.

It must be remembered that outside the Gold Rush region a dollar had such greater value that these amounts of money must be at least quadrupled to come even close to their real value. Outside the camp areas you could get a good hotel room for a dollar and a suite for two dollars. A loaf of bread cost a dime and a complete meal fifteen cents. At almost any saloon a nickel glass of beer would quench your thirst and sandwiches at the free-lunch counter would quell your hunger. Ah, the good old days!

It was a much different story in the Gold Rush country. Storekeepers, hotel owners and suppliers of mining tools charged exorbitant prices. A few miners attained wealth, but most left as poor as they had arrived. With hands that had never known toil and muscles that had never known pain, the merchants and dealers ended up with the gold.

In some of the hotels bread sold for a dollar a slice, and if you were in an extravagant mood you could get butter on your slice for another dollar. Eggs, when available, cost five dollars each. A potato set you back another dollar. We kid you not!

But the bed and the sandbars of the Yuba were wielding astonishing wealth. Though the normal was from 24 to 29 ounces a day, Downie and his companions were recovering 40 or more.

Near the Downie camp was a storekeeper named Bill Slater. In the midst of his shenanigans with his customers, he became seriously ill. Major Downie was a good-hearted man who lived by the Golden Rule. He took time off from his gold-seeking to nurse Slater back to health. Downie had formed a partnership with a fellow Scot, Jim Rose, who carried on the mining labor while Downie was occupied.

Slater recovered. And how he recovered! His wife, living in Sacramento, sent word to her husband that they were paying $22 an ounce there for gold instead of the standard $16. He offered to return the major's kindness by taking his gold to Sacramento and collecting the higher prices. Downie agreed, and gave him about $25,000 in gold plus an extra poke for his wife by way of appreciation. Word spread among the nearby camps and others gave Slater their gold to get in on this good deal.

After a round of handshakes, Slater took off to never be seen again in the diggings. Months later a man arriving at Downie's camp looked up the major. "Met a man down in Panama with the name of Bill Slater," he said. "He was crossing the Isthmus with his new wife on his way to Europe. He said you were one of the best fellows in the world and always ready to help a stranger."

"So, that's what he said, did he!" Major Downie then voiced his opinion of Slater. We are forced to note that his statements are unprintable. They would scorch the paper, and we are attempting to write a book that could be read aloud at family gatherings with embarrassment.

Slowly the collection of camps became a town with permanent buildings, streets and a business district. Despite being seventy miles from the main source of supply, forty miles of which were dangerous mountain trails, the population grew to 5,000 in two years. Along narrow Main Street, horses were tethered at night to posts holding up the wooden awnings. Boardwalks lighted by rays from kerosene lamps shining through windows were crowded by booted men.

In time there was a theatre where the present movie house now stands. Here Edwin Booth, Lola Montez, Lottie Crabtree and other stars of the day entertained the show-hungry residents. They were rewarded with coins and gold pokes thrown onto the stage.

And there is the Costa Store. It was built in 1853 of uncemented shale with walls four-feet thick at the base and 27 scales still being used to weigh gold dust and nugget. Gold still is occasionally mined around Downieville, but it is increasingly difficult to find and ever more difficult to extract.

Many old buildings remain, as does the ancient cemetery, and the flowing Yuba River over who's bridge the only women hung during the gold rush met her end. Her legend and fretful spirit remains today.

JUANITA
Disgraceful Death
In Downieville.

A word about the ladies. God bless them. In the beginning there were no women in the camps. Then slowly some Mexican women drifted into the region as it became more permanent. The first Yankee woman to appear was Signora Elise Biscaccianti, a noted pianist of her day. She was welcomed by a large crowd of men whose cheers echoed and re-echoed from the steep-walled canyons of the Yuba. She was then carried on men's shoulders, as was her piano, to the finest quarters available.

There followed, of course, the camp followers of varied races. In the early days the scarcity of women was a hardship almost unendurable. The appearance of a woman brought miners from miles around just to look at her and follow her around. Women reminded the men of their faraway homes, of the families they left behind.

As the camps became towns, brothels were established along with gambling houses and the ever-present saloons. But, as one writer states, "Generally speaking, the lowest of harlots was treated as respectfully as any pillar of the community."

At many of the camps there was more than one reason for this. They not only satisfied men's sexual needs, but many doubled as nurses. Sickness was frequent. The miners' diet of beans, sow-belly (salt port) and saleratus bread, with occasional flapjacks, frequently caused scurvy. Only fruit, green vegetables and fresh meat, all rare in the region could have prevented these cases, although the strenuous physical labor of some healthy miners enabled them to escape the curse. So rare was fruit that one man paid a thousand dollars for a tiny plot with two apple trees.

So the stereotype of the prostitute with a kind, loving heart truly existed in the camps. They were friends. When they died crowds of grateful men attended the funerals and burials. Sometimes fences were erected around the graves. A few became legends in the annals of the West.

Only after 1855 when men began to bring their wives and lady-friends to the camps and towns did the plague of scurvy start to end. The women planted gardens to raise green vegetables, and insisted that their men had proper diets.

But there is on Downieville's rich and colorful history a blot, a shadow, the unforgotten memory of one particular crime. For it was Downieville where the only women during the gold-rush was lynched.

Accounts of the short and tragic life of Juanita have been subject to distortion as it was told and retold through the years. Therefore, we are indebted to William B. Secrest, author of the booklet <u>Juanita</u> (Saga-West Publishing Co, Fresno,CA.1967).

He laboriously went back to the original and contemporary media and examined reports of what really happened. The reconstructed conversation in this chapter is based on eye-witness accounts and testimony recorded at the trial as ascertained by Secrest.

All accounts agree that Juanita was an attractive young Hispanic woman aged about 24. According to Major Downie, "She was of the Spanish-Mexican mixture, proud and self-possessed, her bearing graceful, almost majestic. She was, in the miners' parlance, 'well put up'." She was not a prostitute, but was living with her paramour, a slightly-built Mexican named Jose.

It was July 4, 1851. California had joined the Union the year before and this would be the town's first Fourth-of-July celebration. Thousands of miners came into town from the outlying camps. Flags were displayed everywhere. A platform had been built for the speakers of the day led by John D. Weller, later to be governor of California. There were bands and parades.

But it was booze that lubricated the occasion--barrels of it that flowed like a mighty flood through the numerous saloons.

Lights and shadows punctuated the bizarre scene as thousands of miners staggered through the streets shouting and brawling. All afternoon the wild celebration continued. By late afternoon sober men were as scarce as fugitive criminals at a policemen's ball. The revelry went on into the night illuminated by whale-oil lamps.

There was probably no man more popular in the Downieville camps than Fred Cannon. He was a born leader, ruggedly handsome and chauvinistic. His impersonations were delightfully entertaining.

As the evening festivities continued, the miners collected into groups and held parties. At one such gathering, Cannon recited one of his most hilarious monologues--a quarrel between a Chinese father, his daughter and her lover, imitating the voices of the characters.

It was past midnight when Cannon left the

group. Leaving with Cannon were two friends, Charley Getzler and Ted Lawson. They proceeded to walk through the town on the board sidewalk singing ribald songs.

When they came to the front of Juanita's shack, Cannon fell against the door, ripping it from its leather hinges and throwing him onto the floor inside. Laughing, he picked up a scarf lying on the floor, scrambled to his feel and tied the scarf around his neck. Lawson later testified that he told Cannon to put it back.

Secrest writes: "What happened at this moment is a disputed point in California history. Some maintained that Cannon intentionally broke down the door with the idea of making advances to Josefa (Secrest uses the woman's Spanish name throughout his text, but has her anglicized name in his book's title.) It was even asserted that he had been fruitlessly pursuing her for some time, but that she had spurned his attentions. Whatever the truth, it is definitely known that Josefa was in the room when Cannon stumbled in. Getzler's story was that he told Cannon to put the scarf back and that as soon as they saw Josefa, they put the door back in place and left. The drunken miners staggered off down the street and after a few ribald comments laughingly forgot the incident."

Dawn heralded a new day destined to be the last in Juanita's short life. About mid-morning Cannon and Lawson appeared in front of the home and office of Dr. William Hunter which was located next door to Juanita's small shanty. Lawson testified later that they came to get some medication for Cannon. While they were talking to the doctor they were joined by Jose, Juanita's live-in lover.

"Senor Cannon," said Jose, "you busted my door down last night and you must pay me for it."

Cannon turned and regarded the small Mexican with annoyance. "I did not bust your door," he said. "Your door was so flimsy a passing dog could knock it down. Let's take a look at your damn door."

When the two men approached the door, Juanita came out, her features contorted with anger and speaking rapidly in Spanish. Cannon frowned. "Take it easy," he replied. "Why make such a fuss over a little thing like this?"

Jose put his hand inside his coat. "Don't you dare pull a knife on me, Mex," Cannon said, "or I'll knock you down flat as a rug."

"No knife," Jose explained. "I won't fight you. You're too big and strong. Just pay me something for my broken door."

By this time a group of spectators had stopped and were listening to the argument. "I've got no more time to argue about this," Cannon insisted. "I got better things to do."

Still speaking excitedly in Spanish, Juanita moved between the two men. Jose seized her arm and tried to pull her toward the door. "That's right," Cannon said to Jose. "Take your whore inside and shut her up."

Jose managed to get her to the doorway. Cannon's remark now drove Juanita's already intense anger to a fever pitch. "I am not a whore," she shouted, her dark eyes flashing. "Don't you dare call me bad names. Come inside my house and call me that!"

At that instant Juanita was standing inside the doorway. Jose was behind her. Lawson was standing behind Cannon who was in front of the door. Cannon had no intention of allowing the spectators to see a pair of Mexicans win the argument and he was trying to calm her down. Juanita seized

193

a knife from a table just inside the door and stepping forward plunged it into Cannon's chest. Cannon staggered back and fell into the arms of Lawson. His eyes widened with surprise as a crimson stain appeared on his shirt. "That bitch stabbed me," he half whispered as his knees buckled.

Juanita suddenly realized the gravity of her thoughtless, impulsive act. It was her fiery Latin temper that was to seal her grim fate.. With a short scream she turned and fled to the Craycroft Saloon where Jose was employed as a card dealer. Jose followed her trailed by a number of witnesses.

Lawson and several friends carried Cannon to the doctor's office next door. Cannon was growing weaker by the second. There was no hope. The knife blade had penetrated Cannon's heart. Lying on a couch, he drew his final breath and died.

At the saloon some of the startled gamblers tried to hide the woman. Her pursuers, however, were too close behind her. The enraged miners apprehended both Juanita and Jose. Meanwhile, news of the murder spread like a bush fire along the streets and through the camps. Crowds gathered in front of the doctor's office and the Craycroft Tavern. Juanita and Jose were taken to a log cabin on the side of the plaza near the speaker's platform. Cannon's body was taken to a large tent and placed on display. He was wearing a red flannel shirt unbuttoned to expose the wound on his chest. The exhibition only served to increase the anger of the visitors

About two hours after the stabbing, Juanita and Jose were marched to the speaker's platform where Senator Weller had spoken the previous day. Around the platform an unruly mob of men pushed and shoved, many drunk, and wanting her to be hung immediately. A statement that was overpowering, often unfair, but unfortunately true was rung through the crowd here in Downieville. "Lets be reasonable" one drunk spectator said. "Lets give them a fair trial and THEN we'll hang um!"

The appointed a man named Jim Rose as the trial judge. Twelve jurors were chosen and one William Spear selected as prosecutor. Two lawyers, Pickett and Brocklebank, were appointed defense counsel. Another lawyer by the name of Thayer protested the informal trial. Voicing his opinion that the hostile blood thirsty mob was out for blood. Surely there could not be a fair trial for Juanita and Jose. He was pulled from the platform and the mob attacked him. According to an eye witness, George Barton, Thayer was beaten by the enraged miners as they dragged him several hundred feet. There he was dropped, bloody and in a heap, at the far edge of the crowd. Another eye witness, David Barstow, whose manuscript is in the Bancroft Library in Berkeley, California, noted the miners were "the hungriest, craziest, wildest mob standing around that I ever saw anywhere."

Witnesses were called. The first, a twelve year old boy named Frank stated he was present at the stabbing and that Juanita seemed very angry and determined.

Following was Dr. Hunter who had pronounced Cannon dead. He stated he had not seen the stabbing but knew Cannon to be a "remarkably athletic but peaceful man." Ted Lawson, on his friends behalf, stated that Cannon was calm and collected, where as Juanita acted with "a great deal of temper and determination."

Judge Rose stood up. "I'm sorry lady," he said. "The time has come." Juanita began her final walk with two guards holding her arms so she could not flee.

The scaffold was built of a wide plank held four feet above the wooden Jersey bridge. It spanned the Yuba River below. A rope with a noose was then tied to the structure.

According to the <u>Pacific</u> <u>Star</u> newspaper, "At the time appointed for the execution, the prisoner was taken to the gallows, which she approached without the least trepidation. She said, while standing by the gallows, so I was informed, that she had killed the man Cannon, and expected to suffer for it; that the only request she had to make was, that after she had suffered, her body should be given to her friends, in order that she might be decently interred.

"This request was promptly complied with (and) she extended her hand to each of the bystanders immediately around her, and bidding each an 'adios senor,' voluntarily ascended the scaffold, took the rope and adjusted it around her neck with her own hand, releasing her luxuriant black hair from beneath it so that it should flow free.

"Her arms were then pinioned, to which she strongly objected, her clothes tied down, the cap adjusted over her face, and in a moment more the cords which supported the scaffolding had been cut, and she hung suspended between the heavens and earth."

As the unruly crowd realized it was over, some were remorseful. "What have we done!" one man stated. They slowly left the scene, many to drown their memories in whiskey from one of the many bars and saloons. Behind them the tiny body of a beautiful Mexican woman swung in the breeze. It was several hours later, in the dark of evening, that some townsfolk cut her body down, and delivered it to the home of one of her friends.

The bodies of Juanita and Cannon, the slayer and the slain, were interred side by side in the Downieville cemetery. We wonder if they are fighting still. Disturbing also, in 1870 the Downieville Cemetery was moved to a new location to permit the site to be searched for gold. A local historian, George Barton, writes that at that time Juanita's skull was stolen.

The wooden Jersey bridge was washed away in a flood years ago. In it's place a new modern steel bridge was constructed. The plaque reads: IN MEMORY OF JUANITA- THE SPANISH WOMAN, LYNCHED BY MOB FROM ORIGINAL BRIDGE ON THIS SITE JULY 5, 1851. Downieville remembers!

Cannon either went to his final reward, or chooses not to show himself to the town that saw his demise. Juanita, however chooses to linger, in the hills, in the fields, and on the bridge. Psychically sensitive residents and visitors have observed the apparition of Juanita. Some are startled, some are frightened, and all wonder why she cannot find peace.

According to former Downieville resident Mary Hansford, "I once worked in one of the stores in the community," she told us. "As I became acquainted, many people told of seeing the ghostly Juanita,but I thought they were superstitious. After all, this is a small town with very close people. I figured it was a story passed on from one generation to another to scare the children. I was quite startled a few months ago when my car broke down. I decided to walk home because it was such a beautiful clear night.

"When I came to the Downieville bridge, I saw what appeared to be fog in one corner. As I approached, I saw the face of Juanita. She was dressed as one would be long ago. She was silently uttering words, trying to tell me something.

"I was frightened and backed away, but I guess I didn't have to. She seemed no

longer aware of my presence. She looked
up, closed her eyes, and disappeared. Just
like that! I can positively affirm that I
saw her. I am no longer a skeptic."

James Kellog also saw Juanita. "When I
was a lad I could expect to see her every
now and then, and I still do. We can do
nothing for her, but most townsfolk have
learned to take her in their stride. I hope
someday she will find peace."

There are parapsychologists that tell us
that hauntings can be caused by extreme
emotional energy experienced by people long
gone. Therefore, they hypothesize, certain
locales have built up their own
"atmospheres" over the years. These auras
can be felt by sensitive persons who
encounter these remnants caught in the web
of time. Our psychics repeatedly tried to
reason with Juanita, and release her from
this reality. They failed. Juanita chooses
to stay in Downieville, as do many spirits
in all the old towns of the Gold Rush
Country.

15

MAPS

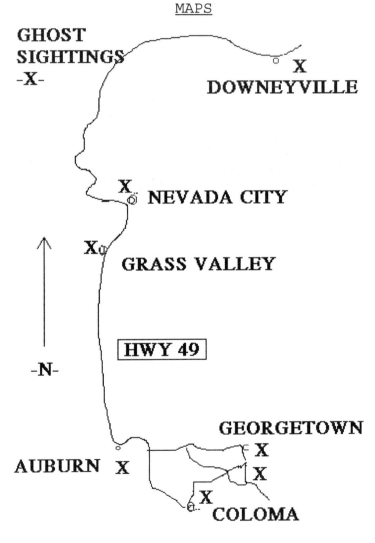

GHOST
SIGHTINGS
-X-

X
DOWNEYVILLE

X
NEVADA CITY

X
GRASS VALLEY

↑

-N-

HWY 49

GEORGETOWN
X

X

AUBURN   X

X
COLOMA

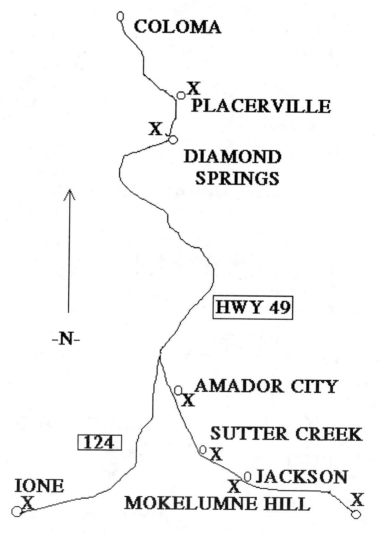

COLOMA

X
PLACERVILLE

X
DIAMOND
SPRINGS

-N-

HWY 49

AMADOR CITY
X

SUTTER CREEK
X

124

JACKSON

IONE
X

X
MOKELUMNE HILL

X

16

ABOUT THE AUTHOR, THE BOOK, AND VIDEO

Nancy Bradley is the author of three books and over two thousand articles appearing in major newspapers, magazines, and other publications, both Nationally and Internationally. These publications include: Good Housekeeping, Guideposts, Dog Fancy, and California Highway Patrolman. She is responsible for the breaking of many stories of International appeal such as her blockbuster headline: "Over 12,000 Convicted Drunk Drivers Piloting Private Airplanes." This story was instrumental in getting FAA and congressional investigations leading to legislation and regulations regarding new restrictions on private pilots. A former member of California Press Women, the National League of American Pen Women, International Press,U.P., A.P.I., and Interpress of London & New York, Ms. Bradley has interviewed and investigated many issues concerning government and the motion picture industry, and is also sought by top publications to decipher, research and report stories concerning the mysteries of nature, psychic phenomena, ghosts and UFO's. Considered an expert in these fields, it was during her work with a National publication that she uncovered the unexpected and unexplainable large group of ghost sightings within the Gold Rush Country. This research lead to her book Gold Rush Ghosts and now the updated

Incredible World of Gold Rush Ghosts. Although the first Gold Rush Ghosts was a national best seller, after ten years, it is now off the shelves. A few copies are still available from the author.

The former beauty contest winner, professional dancer, model, talk show guest, and recipient of many writing awards, now resides in the Heart of California's Gold Rush Country. There she and her husband Robert share their Placerville home with her long time companion and protector-Bear (The 110 lb Chesapeake Bay) and her (Not always so friendly) Bobtail cat, Loner. They enjoy long visits with her grown children, Robert and Robin King,(Both accomplished in their own right) and a multitude of friends dating from her high school days to the present.

TBR: Is the coming together of three long time friends to put into works, The Incredible World of Gold Rush Ghosts. The initials TBR is a mystery to anyone except the three, but they welcome anyone's guess with smiles.

A Video of The Incredible World of Gold Rush Ghosts will become available Nationally in the not to distant future. For more information or to place your name on a waiting list please write:

Gold Rush Ghosts
P.O. Box 911
Diamond Springs, CA. 95619

Rosemary Dean and Pat Kenyon do their stuff during the invertigation for the <u>Incredible World</u> <u>of</u> <u>Gold</u> <u>Rush</u> <u>Ghosts.</u>

For further information on the amazing psychic powers of Rosemary "Rosie" Dean, see <u>Kicking</u> <u>and</u> <u>Fighting</u> <u>All</u> <u>The</u> <u>Way</u> the first in a series of <u>Rosie</u> <u>Books</u> also written by Nancy Bradley.

Mail to Psychics Rosemary Dean or Pat Kenyon can be sent <u>C/O:</u>

<u>GOLD</u> <u>RUSH</u> <u>GHOSTS</u>
P.O. Box 911
Diamond Springs,CA. 95619

For appointments Ms. Dean can be reached at:
(530) 626-5138.

For appointments Pat Kenyon can be reached at: (530) 677-6851

<u>GOLD</u> <u>RUSH</u> <u>GHOSTS</u> is always interested in true stories of ghostly encounters, U.F.O's, or other cases of the strange and unknown. If you have a story you would like to share or explore, please contact Nancy Bradley, Robert Reppert or Dan Amos at:
<u>GOLD</u> <u>RUSH</u> <u>GHOSTS</u>
P.O. Box 911
Diamond Springs, CA. 95619

<u>GOLD</u> <u>RUSH</u> <u>GHOSTS</u> Psychic Center is available to research phenomena, and identify ghosts in your home, surroundings, and around you as a person.

For talk show interviews, book signings, subscriptions to the <u>Gold</u> <u>Rush</u> <u>Ghosts</u> newsletter, appointments   or   other information call:
<u>GOLD</u> <u>RUSH</u> <u>GHOSTS</u>
(530) 622-0977

GOLD RUSH GHOSTS

PO BOX 911 DIAMOND SPRINGS 95619

530-622-0977

ORDER FORM
MAIL ORDERS TO THE ADDRESS ABOVE

ADRESS OF CUSTOMER

PAYMENT BY

Check	
Credit card number	VISA []
	MASTER CARD []
	SIGNATURE

EXP DATE

ITEM NO.		QTY.	UNIT COST	TOTAL AMOUNT
1	GOLD RUSH GHOSTS		9.95	
2	THE INCREDIBLE WORLD OF GOLD RUSH GHOSTS		12.95	
3				
			SUBTOTAL	
			Shipping charges	2.00 PER ITEM
	Ordered by	7.25 %	Tax	
			TOTAL DUE	

SPECIAL INSTRUCTIONS